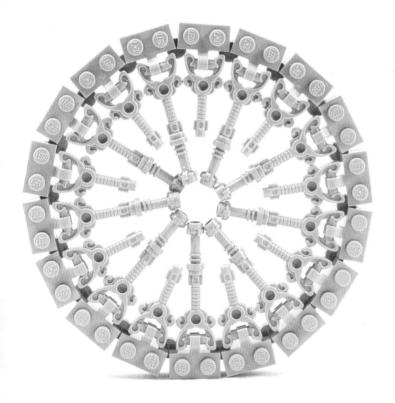

THE LEGO® ARCHITECTURE IDEA BOOK

1001 IDEAS FOR BRICKWORK, SIDING,
WINDOWS, COLUMNS, ROOFING,
AND MUCH, MUCH MORE!

ALICE FINCH

SAN FRANCISCO

The LEGO® Architecture Idea Book. Copyright © 2018 by Alice Finch.

All rights reserved. No part of this work may be reproduced or transmitted in any form or by any means, electronic or mechanical, including photocopying, recording, or by any information storage or retrieval system, without the prior written permission of the copyright owner and the publisher.

Printed in China

First printing

22 21 20 19 18   1 2 3 4 5 6 7 8 9

ISBN-10: 1-59327-821-7
ISBN-13: 978-1-59327-821-2

Publisher: William Pollock
Production Editor: Serena Yang
Cover Design: Mimi Heft
Interior Design and Composition: Serena Yang
Developmental Editor: Annie Choi
Proofreader: Emelie Burnette

For information on distribution, translations, or bulk sales, please contact No Starch Press, Inc. directly:

No Starch Press, Inc.
245 8th Street, San Francisco, CA 94103
phone: 1.415.863.9900; info@nostarch.com; www.nostarch.com

Library of Congress Cataloging-in-Publication Data
LC record available at https://lccn.loc.gov/2017050208

To builders everywhere:
Every day I am inspired to create
because of your fresh ideas, impressive
modeling techniques, innovative MOCs,
and outside-the-box thinking.

About the Author

Alice Finch is a renowned LEGO builder whose creations include large-scale models of Hogwarts Castle and Rivendell. Her work has been featured on NPR, in the documentary *A LEGO Brickumentary*, and in *The Huffington Post*, *WIRED*, and *The Seattle Times*. When Alice is not building models in her LEGO room in Seattle, WA, she travels all over the world, giving talks, demonstrating building techniques, and teaching builders of all ages how to use bricks to make the world a better place.

Contents

Preface

I remember building with basic LEGO bricks as a child. My natural tendency, even then, was to build architectural structures. My dad is a general contractor, so I grew up around the building process, surrounded by unusual woodworking projects like a convex front door. I suspect my early exposure to building projects trained me to see the little details in architecture everywhere. When I travel, I always have a camera in hand to capture interesting and often quirky designs. Maybe I'll get a few odd looks when snapping a photo of what appears to be a boring wall, but if there's an interesting detail, I want to document it.

In addition to finding inspiration in real-world architecture, I am motivated by the LEGO community and the models I see at conventions, in workshops, and on blog posts. There are so many phenomenal builders who stretch the repertoire of how bricks can be used, not just in architectural models but in the LEGO world as a whole. It's important to acknowledge the influence of other people's ideas, even when they may be unconsciously absorbed. So to all the builders out there, thank you for contributing to the collective creative wisdom of this community. I am grateful to everyone who may have contributed, even in the slightest way, to a light-bulb moment. It is the collective creativity of us all that keeps this hobby fresh and inspiring.

About This Book

I hope that builders of all ages and experiences will find this book to be a useful tool and a source of inspiration. Just as a writer consults a thesaurus to find more interesting words, you can use this book to incorporate more interesting and detailed architectural elements into your buildings.

Identifying Parts

There are thousands of different LEGO parts and many different online catalogs and references. Unfortunately, the naming and part numbering systems used by these catalogs are not universal, obvious, or logical. I have tried to find a happy medium when identifying parts used in the models, using the following convention:

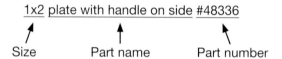

Size: Some catalogs reverse the size format for certain parts. For example, BrickLink (*https://www.bricklink.com/*) lists slopes as 4x2 instead of 2x4. If the size doesn't seem to make sense, try reversing it.

Part Name: Names are made as concise and clear as possible. Printed parts and stickers have extremely long names, so many are referenced by what sets they come in.

Part Number: Some catalogs differentiate between many different versions of a part. Molds have changed over the decades, so sometimes a part will have identifiers like *a*, *b*, or *c* at the end of the number. I omit these identifiers, as it usually doesn't matter which version it is. When it does matter, I make a note of it.

Some parts have versions with distinct numbers, such as 1x2 jumper plates, which come in two different versions. The main difference between the versions is whether the bottom has a post that fits into the center of an open stud (#3794) or three equal divided stud holders (#15573).

Custom Parts

For just the right look, sometimes only a custom part will do. I've used custom pieces or printing from the following vendors: altBricks (*http://altbricks.com/*), BrickArms (*http://brickarms.com/*), BrickForge (*http://brickforge.com/*), Brickstuff (*http://brickstuff.com/*), BrickWarriors (*http://brickwarriors.com/*), Citizen Brick (*https://citizenbrick.com/*), Jolly Viking Bricks (*http://jollyvikingbricks.com/*), and PromoTec (*http://promotecinc.com/*).

How-to Models

When it's difficult to see the building techniques used in the finished model, look at the color-coded how-to box that shows what parts are being used and how.

Experimenting

Each model serves as an inspiration only. If you don't have the same exact part in a certain color, use a different part or color. Be inspired, but don't be afraid to modify a technique to fit your needs and improvise with parts you already have in your stash.

Acknowledgments

Creating a book is a massive undertaking that I could not have done without the support of many other people.

To Reiner: The first gift you ever gave me was a LEGO set. Little did we know just how much LEGO building would become part of our family and transform from a hobby into a professional undertaking. Thank you for building with us, for not minding our LEGO room taking over our house, and for being a supporter and partner in all that I do.

To Thorin and Hadrian: Thank you for getting me back into building and inspiring me with your clever, quirky, and imaginative creations. You impress me with your ability to build detailed, functioning models.

To my family: Thank you for providing the bins of bricks when I was a kid, for exposing me to the finer points of architecture, and for understanding and encouraging me on this adventure.

Thanks also to Kim, Robin, and Megan for supporting me in my endeavors and being an important part of my village.

Thank you to my building colleagues in ArchLUG for sharing your expertise and innovative techniques and contributing to our many collaborative efforts, and to SeaLUG for making me aware of the Adult Fans of LEGO (AFOL) community and the friendships and support that it can offer.

Models in this book were inspired by Bruce Lowell, Katie Walker, Siercon and Coral, Simon NH, Soren Hixenbaugh, and many others.

Thank you to all of the minifigs at No Starch Press for all of your many contributions in bringing this book to fruition. An enormous thank you to Serena for juggling thousands of photographs, captions, and part details and patiently wrangling them into manageable chapters. It has been a tremendous privilege to work with you in shaping this book.

Brickwork

Simple Brick Walls

Use modified bricks to create wall variations and patterns. Texture can make a monochromatic wall more interesting without using more-complicated techniques.

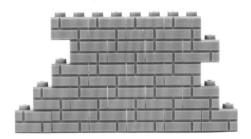

1x2 modified brick with masonry profile #98283

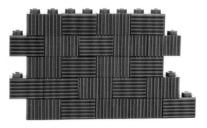

1x2 modified brick with grill #2877

1x2 jumper plate #3794/#15573

1x2 modified log brick #30136

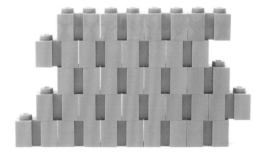

1x2 modified brick with groove #4216

2x2 modified brick with sloped end #47457

Decorative Relief

Raised tiles, hinge bricks, and hinge plates add texture to plain surfaces, creating decorative relief patterns.

Raised tiles add interest to a monochromatic wall. The wall can be set back on jumper plates (left) or flush (right).

Raised 1x2 tiles (#3069) add texture to 1x2 modified bricks with masonry profile (#98283), and a subtle color contrast adds interest.

The bump of the hinge bricks (#3830 with #3831) creates the look of irregular bricks that can be arranged randomly or in a pattern.

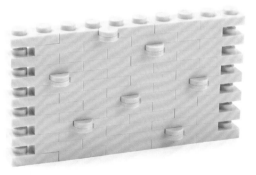

Hinge plates (#2429 with #2430) create a similar texture.

Quoins

A quoin is an architectural element used to accentuate masonry blocks at exterior corners of a wall. They can be overlapping or non-overlapping.

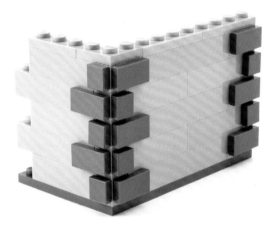

Set two 1x1 bricks with stud on side (#87087) together but with the studs facing in different directions to create non-overlapping quoins.

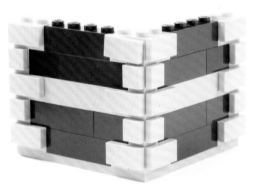

Or simply use a 1x1 brick with studs on 2 adjacent sides (#26604).

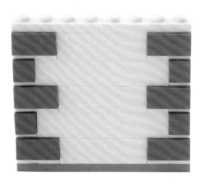

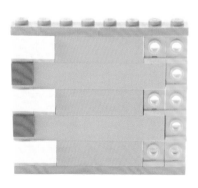

Use headlight bricks (#4070) to set tiles back into the wall for a subtler quoin effect.

You can also build quoins using textured bricks or even gold bar pieces (#99563).

Alternating 1x1 bricks (#3005) with 1x1 round bricks (#3062) creates a subtle quoin.

How To: Overlapping Quoins

Because 1x2 tiles (#3069) do not have any stud holders, you can slide the tile over to cover the depth of the 1x1 tile (#3070).

You can use either a 1x1 brick with studs on 2 adjacent sides (#26604), as shown on the left, or a 1x1 brick with studs on 4 sides (#4733) placed next to a 1x1 Technic brick (#6541), as shown on the right.

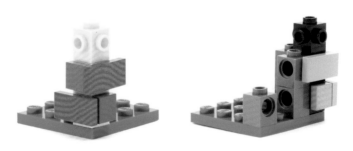

Stone Facade Walls

Use tiles on a background wall to create a raised facade. The background wall can be a solid color, creating a grout effect, or mixed to look aged and mossy.

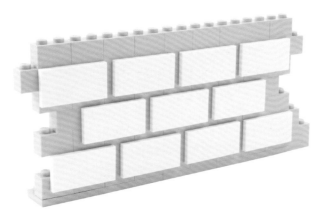

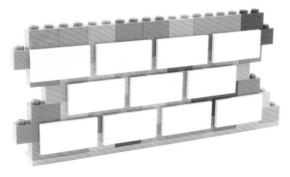

Mix colors to make a mottled background.

How To

The back of the wall shows how the Technic half pins are arranged. To offset the 2x4 tiles, three different types of bricks are used on the front of the wall.

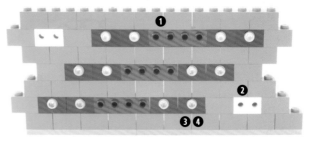

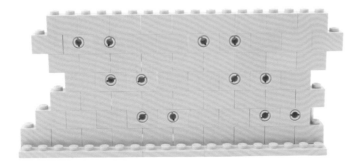

❶ 1x4 brick with 4 studs on side #30414
(or two 1x2 bricks with 2 studs on side #11211)

❷ 1x2 brick with 2 studs on side #11211
(or 1x2 brick with 2 studs on 2 sides #52107)

❸ 1x2 Technic brick #3700

❹ Technic half pin #4274

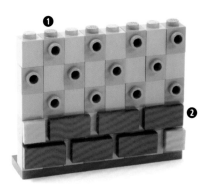

Alternate a brick and a stud to create a pattern with 1x2 tiles. Using contrasting colors makes the bricks behind the tiles look like grout.

❶ 1x1 brick with stud on side #87087
❷ 1x2 tile #3069

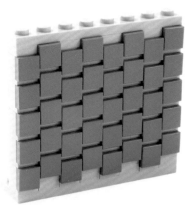

Attach 1x1 tiles to headlight bricks. Offset the headlights by a plate for a nice alternating pattern.

❶ 1x1 headlight brick #4070
❷ 1x1 tile #3070

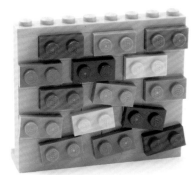

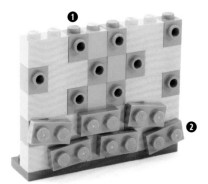

For a wider grout line or to allow tiles or plates to sit at an angle, space the studs out.

❶ 1x1 brick with stud on side #87087
❷ 1x2 plate #3023

Weathered Walls

Use several shades of small plates to mimic discoloration from age and weather. As plates are smaller than bricks, they show changes in color more gradually.

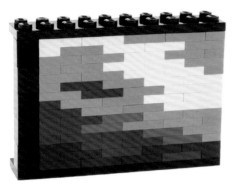

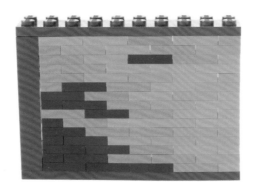

Different color families provide different weathering effects. Use green plates to mimic an old wall covered in moss.

Arrange 1x2 tiles (#3069) and 1x2 jumper plates (#3794/#15573) by recessing some and pushing others out to vary the color and texture.

How To: Choosing the Right Colors

Use a variety of bricks from the same color family to make a simple weathered wall.

❶ Dark orange, medium dark flesh, tan, dark tan, reddish brown, dark brown

❷ Dark blue, sand blue, white, light gray, dark gray, black

❸ Sand green, dark green, olive green

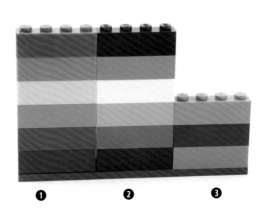

❶   ❷   ❸

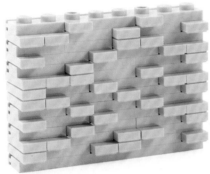

Mix 1x2 jumper plates (#3794/#15573) and 1x2 plates with rail (#32028) for very subtle texture on the front (top) or exaggerated texture on the back (bottom).

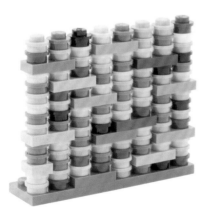

Stacking 1x1 round plates (#4073) makes a pebbled wall. A mix of the natural colors creates variegation, and a few well-spaced 1x2 plates (#3023) hold it all together.

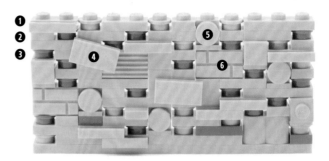

Combine a variety of pieces to build a deteriorating wall.

❶ 1x2 plate with rail #32028

❷ 1x1 plate #3024

❸ 1x1 round plate #4073

❹ 1x2 tile #3069

❺ 1x1 round tile #98138

❻ 1x2 modified brick with masonry profile #98283

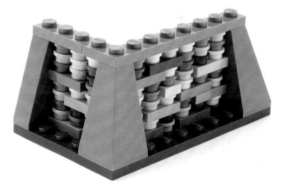

Add 2x2x2 slopes (#3688) to reinforce and emphasize the corners of a pebbled wall.

Crumbling Walls

Crumbling stucco or plaster can reveal the exposed rebar or the masonry underneath.

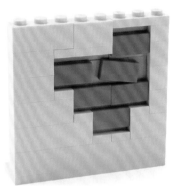

Attach tiles to bricks with studs on side set back on a jumper plate. Attach the tile with one stud if you want it tilted or two studs if you want it straight.

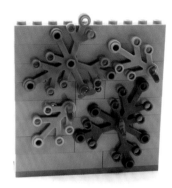

Integrate with vegetation when a building is being reclaimed by the wild or to show climbing vines.

How To: Exposed Rebar

Connect horizontal bars to 1x2 Technic bricks with axle holes (#32064), and fit vertical bars into the open studs of jumper plates on the back row of bricks. The irregular opening created with slopes emphasizes the look.

Or use a combination of #2 axle and pin connectors, Technic bushes, and 3L or 4L axles, bars, or other similar pieces to create the exposed rebar look.

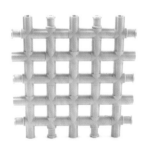
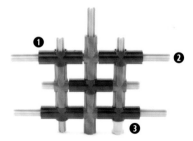

❶ #2 axle and pin connector #32034

❷ 3L axle #4519

❸ Technic bush #3713

Wall Cladding and Shingles

Simple Siding

Tiles have a subtle groove at the bottom that you can use to emphasize gaps between the pieces. Mixing in curved slopes creates even more texture.

Textured Siding

Wood-grain tiles come in a variety of lengths and colors. You can use the same wood-grain tiles to add wainscoting to a particular area of a wall.

Gold bar pieces (#99563) also add an interesting texture.

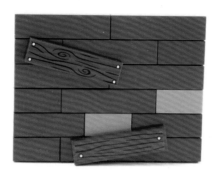

Contrasting Siding

Attaching tiles to 1x2 jumper plates (#3794/#15573) and 2x2 jumper plates (#87580) creates a gap between each row of tiles. Use a contrasting color to emphasize the gap.

Using headlight bricks or bricks with studs on side instead of jumper plates creates a smaller gap.

❶ 1x2 brick with 2 studs on side #11211

❷ 1x1 headlight brick #4070

❸ 1x2 tile #3069

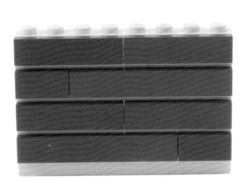

Ramshackle Siding

Interspersing studded bricks with regular bricks gives you room to tilt the tiles, creating a worn-down look.

❶ 1x1 brick with stud on side #87087

❷ 1x4 tile #2431

❸ Various 1x bricks

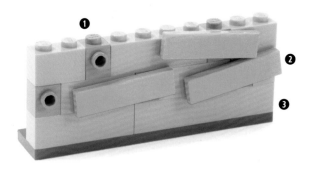

How To

Many of these siding techniques use SNOT (studs not on top) and require building with sideways-facing studs. Here are a few ways to achieve that using bricks and brackets.

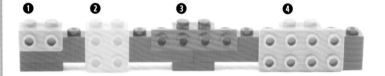

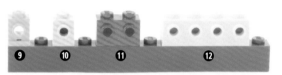

❶ 1x2 - 2x1 bracket #99781

❷ 1x2 - 2x2 bracket #44728

❸ 1x2 - 1x4 bracket #2436

❹ 1x2 - 2x4 bracket #93274

❺ 2x2x2/3 modified plate #99206

❻ 1x2 - 1x2 inverted bracket #99780

❼ 1x2 - 2x2 inverted bracket #99207

❽ 2x2 - 2x2 bracket #3956

❾ 1x1 headlight brick #4070

❿ 1x1 brick with stud on side #87087

⓫ 1x2 brick with 2 studs on side #11211

⓬ 1x4 brick with 4 studs on side #30414

Clapboard Siding

Tiles can also be attached to offset layers of 2x8 plates (#3795), which you can tilt at the base using a hinge to create beveled siding.

❶ 1x4 tile #2431

❷ 1x6 tile #6636

❸ 2x2 hinge brick top #6134

❹ 1x2 hinge brick base #3937

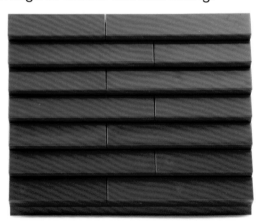

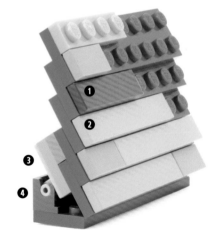

Flat Slope Siding

Standard slopes have a flat lip that creates the look of overlapping siding.

For vertical siding, use a hinge brick (#3937 with #3938 or #6134) to angle the slopes straight up.

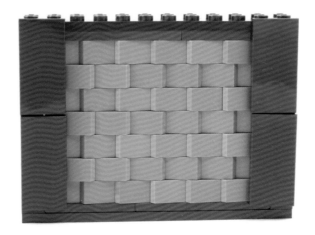

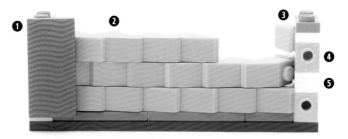

For horizontal siding, alternate layers between supports that hold the layers firmly in place. It also looks good to frame the siding in a contrasting color.

❶ 2x4 tile #87079

❷ 1x2 slope #3040

❸ 1x1 cheese slope #54200

❹ 1x1 brick with stud on side #87087

❺ 1x1 plate #3024

Cheese Slope Siding

Use cheese slopes to make siding or a shingled roof. The slopes can be set at a slightly crooked angle for an aged look thanks to the tolerances between parts.

Use complementary colors for a more random look or use contrasting colors to create a regular pattern.

Using 1x2 cheese slopes creates a smoother profile; the seams between the slopes can be staggered.

Using an occasional slope in another color gives it a weathered look, as if moss were growing on some of the shingles.

How To

Frame the shingles with tiles to make it look different than the same part used on a roof.

- ❶ 1x2 cheese slope #85984
- ❷ 1x1 cheese slope #54200
- ❸ 1x plates
- ❹ 1x4 tile #2431

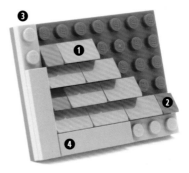

The 1x1 cheese slope comes in a huge variety of colors, with more added every year.

Cheese Slope Roofs

You can tweak this technique to cover not only flat surfaces but also sloping ones.

Attach cheese slopes to
jumper plates for an offset look.

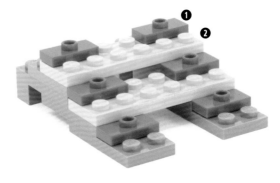

❶ 1x2 jumper plate #3794/#15573

❷ 2x6 plate #3795

To create a smooth surface, use a mix of
plates and bricks so that the cheese slopes
are level with the next row.

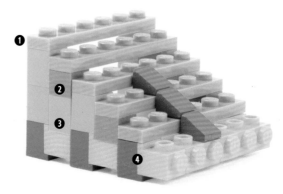

❶ 1x6 plate #3666

❷ 1x1 plate #3024

❸ 1x1 brick #3005

❹ 1x1 headlight brick #4070

Curved Slope Siding

Curved slopes create overlapping patterns that can be either brickwork or woodwork, depending on their color.

1x2 curved slope #11477

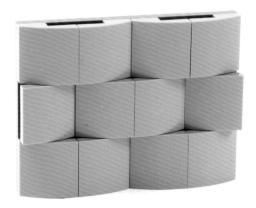

2x2 curved slope #15068

1x3 curved slope #50950

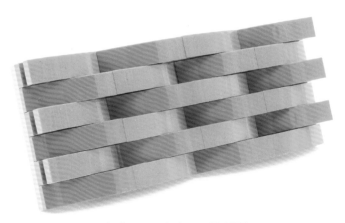

1x4 curved slope #61678

Simple Shingles

Arrange tiles vertically to create shingle patterns for walls and roofs. Tiles can be partially or fully attached.

These tiles are only partially attached, and they're vulnerable to coming off. The bottom layer can be straight or staggered.

These tiles are partially attached on alternating ends.

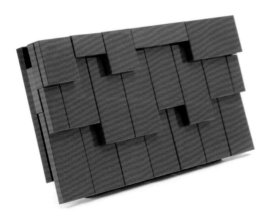

These tiles are fully attached to staggered layers of plates. As you can see, they're flush with the plates and securely attached, though the siding becomes thicker with each layer.

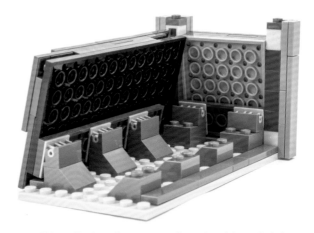

Tilt a tiled wall at an angle using hinge bricks (#3937 with #6134). Putting 2x2 slopes (#3039) under the hinges makes the hinges less likely to get pushed over.

Fishscale Shingles

Round and pentagonal tiles can be used for an entire wall or as a decorative shingle border or feature.

2x4 tile #87079
2x2 round tile #4150/#14769

2x2 round tile #4150/#14769

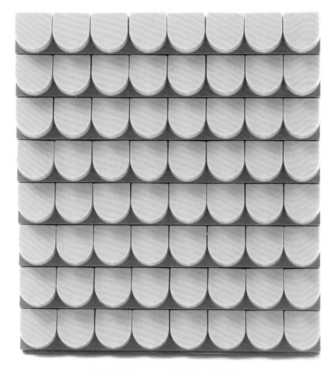

1x1 half rounded tile #24246

2x2 round tile #4150/#14769
2x3 pentagonal tile #22385

2x2 round tile #4150/#14769
2x2 macaroni tile #27925

Fishscale Shingle Roofs

You can use round tiles to cover sloped surfaces as well.

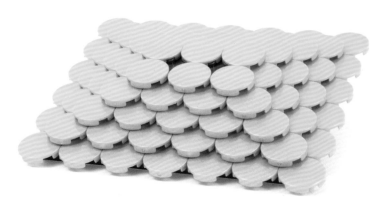

Layer 2x2 round tiles (#4150/#14769)
to create a stepped roof.

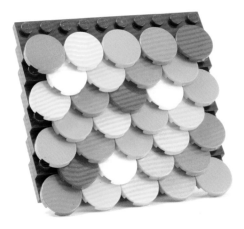

Use colorful tiles for a gingerbread house.

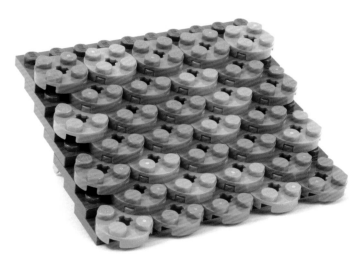

You can achieve a similar look using
2x2 round plates (#4032), which look best when
offset by one stud and with color variation.

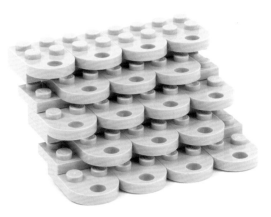

2x3 modified plate with hole #3176

Clip-on Shingles

Tiles with clips create secure shingles that you can stagger to create rustic siding.

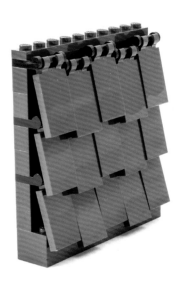

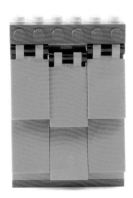

This shingle technique is 2 studs deep. You can cover the edges and corners by stacking 2x2x2 containers (#61780).

How To

Use a 2x4 brick (#3001) on the bottom so that each row of tiles sits at an angle. On the left, a 2x3 tile with 2 clips (#30350) is attached to a 1x2 plate with handle on side (#48336).

You can also stagger the height of shingles using plates, as shown on the right. The first plate with handle (gray) sits three bricks from the bottom. Successive layers of plates are then two bricks apart. Adjacent plates can be staggered up or down one or two plates (lavender).

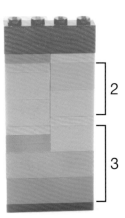

2

3

Clip-on Shingle Roofs

To modify this technique for roofs or other sloped surfaces, you can layer tiles and other flat pieces on staggered plates to create a nice pattern.

2x2 trapezoid flag #44676

2x3 tile with 2 clips #30350
1x2 plate with handle on side #48336

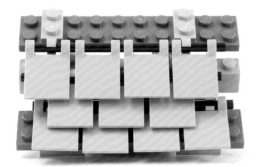

2x2 square flag #2335

2x2 round sign #30261

2x2 triangular sign #892

2x2 square sign #30258

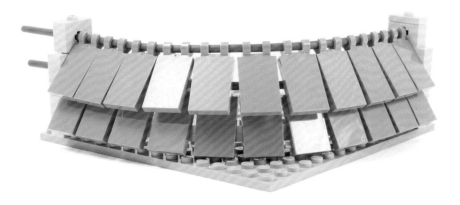

Any of these tiles can attach to handles or to a 3mm soft hose (#bb145).

Curved Shingles

Make a curved shingle wall or roof using rows of 1x2 curved slopes on 2x plates connected to plates with clips and handles.

The curved slopes are staggered to cover the gaps between the plates.

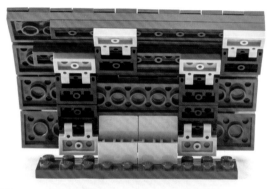

The curved shingles are attached to the base with a hinge brick (#3937 with #6134).

How To

Using 1x2 plates with 2 clips (#60470) and 1x2 plates with handle on side (#48336) makes for a very flexible system for curving a wall at the desired angle without collapse.

❶ 2x plates

❷ 1x2 curved slope #11477

❸ 1x1 cheese slope #54200

❹ 1x4 plate #3710

❺ 1x2 plate with 2 clips #60470

❻ 1x2 plate with handle on side #48336

❼ 1x2 hinge brick base #3937
2x2 hinge brick top #6134

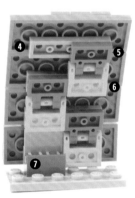

Curved Walls

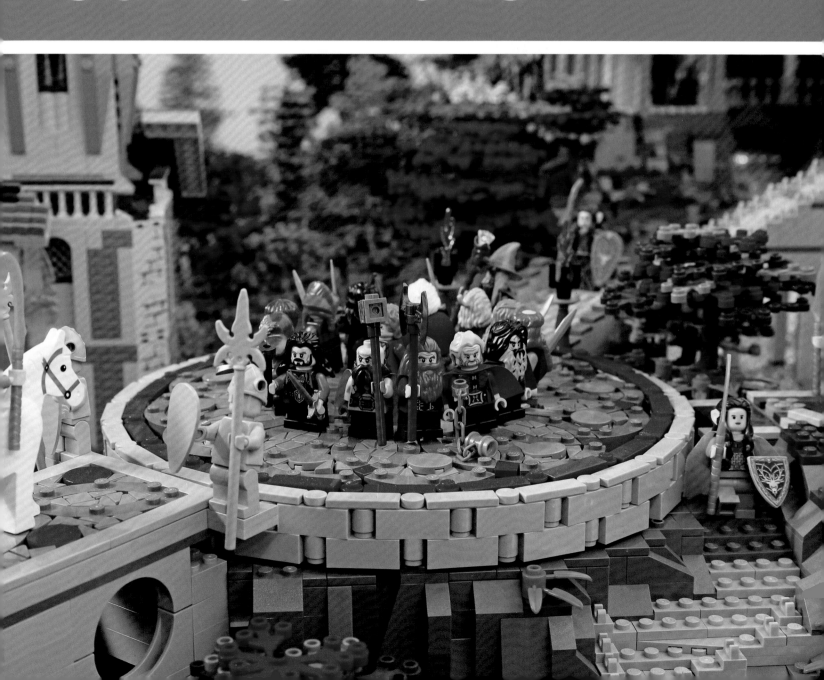

Simple Curved Walls

A wall built with 1x2 bricks (#3004) has enough give that you can bend it slightly. Be careful, though, because forcing too tight of a curve can damage your pieces.

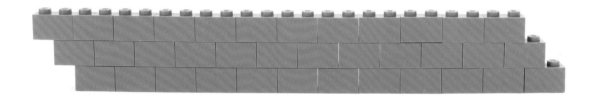

You can also gently bend walls built with 1x2 plates (#3023).

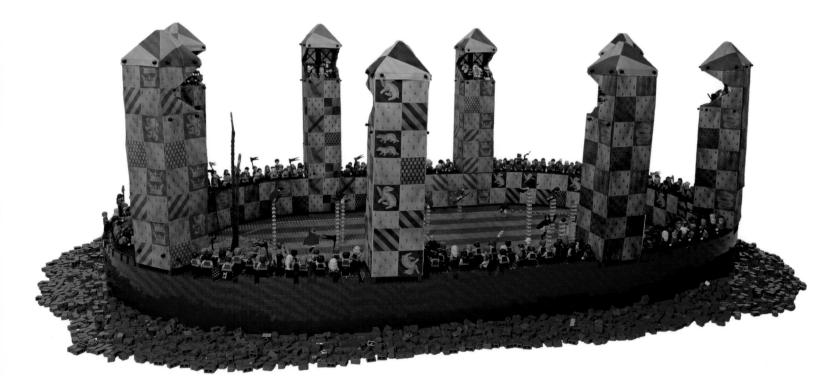

Plate Walls

Alternating 1x2 plates (#3023) with 1x1 round plates (#4073) makes a curved wall. The round plates act like joints: this wall can be bent into a variety of curved shapes.

Use this technique with longer plates or in different colors to create new patterns.

How To

❶ 1x2 plate #3023

❷ 1x1 round plate #4073

Use clear plates to create a curved window.

Brick and Cylinder Walls

You can also use bricks to make a curved wall, using 1x1 round bricks (#3062) as joints.

You can alternate 1x1 round bricks with any type of brick: 1x2 bricks (#3004), 1x3 bricks (#3622), and so on.

Using 1x2 bricks with 2 studs on side (#11211) lets you add cladding to your wall or cover it with vines.

Using 1x4 modified log bricks (#30137) gives your wall a more uniform look.

Bricks with longer lengths will give you walls with larger diameters.

Tiled Brick Walls

Use modified bricks with studs on side and then attach a veneer of tiles. You can even omit the 1x1 round bricks for a different look and more flexibility.

Attach a veneer of tiles to 1x2 bricks with 2 studs on side (#11211) to mimic raised bricks.

Combining 1x1 bricks with stud on side (#87087) with 1x3 plates (#3623) can also create a flexible wall structure.

Skip the round bricks and use just 1x4 bricks with 4 studs on side (#30414). The gaps allow for more flexibility and give the wall a more decrepit look.

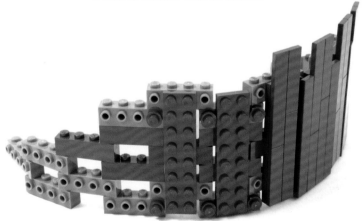

Plates and tiles on the outside can also be attached vertically, which works particularly well when creating a wood exterior.

Grouted Walls

Combine tiles, plates, and bricks to create a bendable wall with distinctive grout lines.

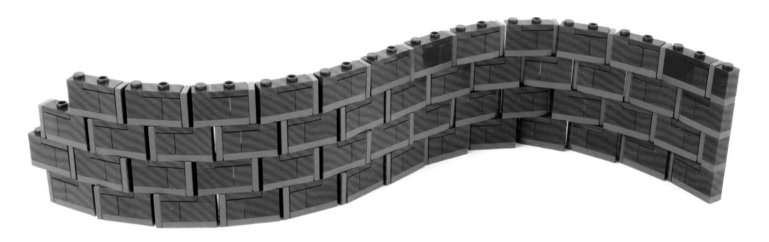

How To

The parts used in this wall are designed with a tiny amount of wiggle room so that they can give slightly when put together. This technique creates just enough give to allow the wall to flex in either direction.

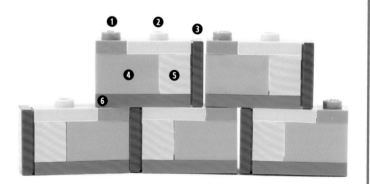

❶ 1x1 plate #3024

❷ 1x2 jumper plate #3794/#15573

❸ 1x2 tile #3069

❹ 1x2 brick #3004

❺ 1x1 brick with stud on side #87087

❻ 1x3 plate #3623

Liftarm Walls

Connecting Technic liftarms with axles can create a rigid wall. Using pins, bars, or hoses as connectors between liftarms makes a flexible wall.

How To

Stagger pins of different lengths to connect liftarms together. Using pins without friction ridges increases the flexibility of your wall.

❶ Pin with friction ridges #2780
   (or pin without friction ridges #3673)

❷ 3L pin #6558

❸ 1x2 liftarm #43857

Liftarms come in both thick and thin varieties. Make a fence by using 1x3 thin liftarms (#6632) and leaving empty spaces between them.

Hinge Walls and Railings

Hinge bricks and plates are very useful for making all kinds of curved walls and railings.

Hinge plates make a good base for balustrades.
Use telescopes as balusters.

❶ 1x2 tile #3069
❷ Telescope #64644
❸ 1x4 hinge plate #2429 with #2430

Keep hinges on one side to create an
arch or alternate the direction of the
hinges to curve a wall in either direction.

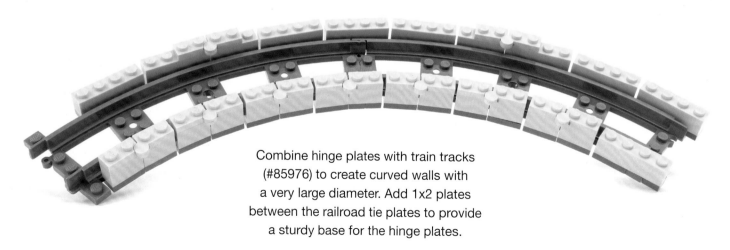

Combine hinge plates with train tracks
(#85976) to create curved walls with
a very large diameter. Add 1x2 plates
between the railroad tie plates to provide
a sturdy base for the hinge plates.

Framing and Paneling

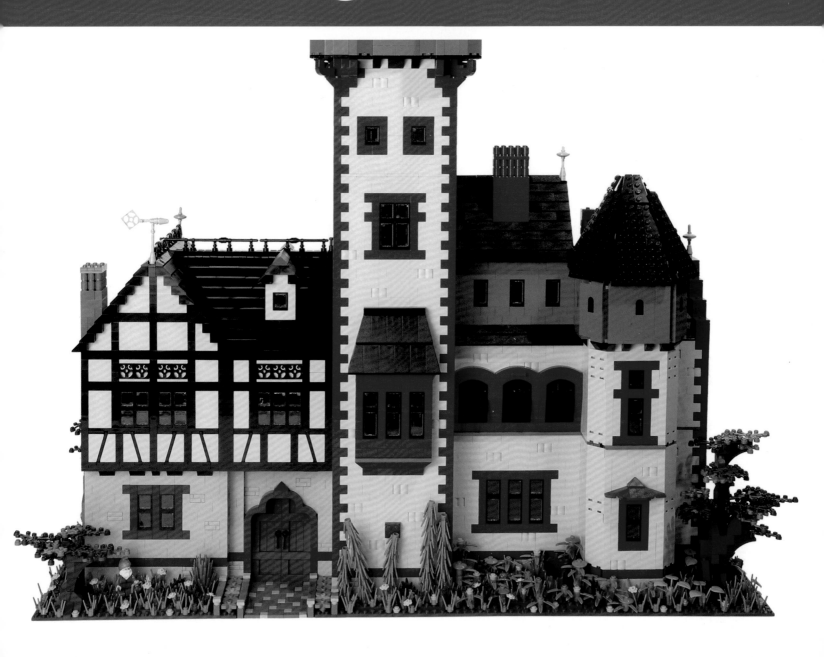

Simple Timber Framing

Half-timbered buildings have striking colors and patterns created by the timbers and the infill, which can be plastered or left exposed.

How To

A 1x4 tile fits perfectly into the slot between a slope and an inverted slope offset by a half stud.

❶ 1x3 plate #3623

❷ 1x1 brick #3005

❸ 1x2 plate #3023

❹ 1x2x3 inverted slope #2449

❺ 1x2x3 slope #4460

❻ 1x2 jumper plate #3794/#15573

❼ 1x1 tile #3070

❽ 1x4 tile #2431

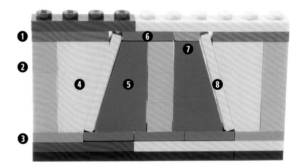

Timber Framing with Masonry

The space between timbers is often left exposed to reveal the infill masonry. You can replicate this masonry with 1x1 cheese slopes and an occasional 1x1 tile.

How To

Although the cheese slopes should fit well enough to stay in with a bit of tension, it's a good idea to reinforce with tape on the back to prevent them from jiggling free. You can also wedge a half pin in the base of the cheese slope to help stabilize the angled 1x1x5 brick.

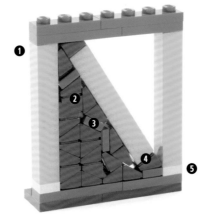

❶ 1x1x5 brick #2453

❷ 1x1 cheese slope #54200

❸ 1x1 tile #3070

❹ Half pin #4274

❺ 1x1 plate #3024

Timber Framing Variations

Many parts can be used to re-create the look of half-timbering. Historic timbered buildings are often brightly colored, so don't feel limited to using brown.

❶ 6L bar with stop ring #63965
   (or 6.6L bar with stop ring #4095)

❷ 1x4 antenna #3957

❸ 4L bar #30374

❹ 3L bar #87994

❺ 8L axle #3707

A bar, antenna, or hose can fit inside this framed space, created using tiles on 1x1 bricks with stud on side (#87087). You can cut longer rigid hose and angle the cut at each end to fit the corner as needed, or bend to form a curved timber frame.

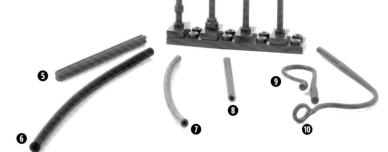

❻ 4mm pneumatic hose #5102 (various lengths)

❼ 3mm soft hose #bb145 (various lengths)

❽ 3mm rigid hose #75 (various lengths)

❾ Whip #88704

❿ Vine #2488

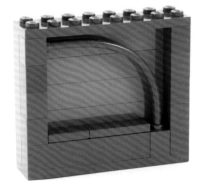

Here, one piece of 3mm rigid hose (#75) makes the complete arch. On each side, the hose is anchored to the bottom with a 1x2 plate with pin hole on top (#11458). At the top of the arch, the hose is inserted through a 1x1 Technic brick (#6541) in the middle divider.

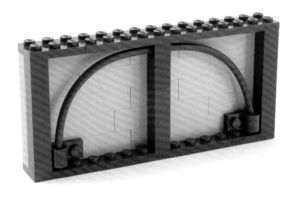

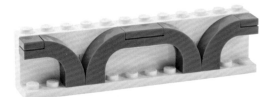

1x3x2 arch with curved top #6005

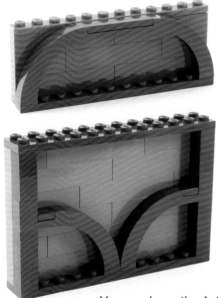

❶ 1x6x2 arch with curved top #6183

❷ 1x2x1 1/3 modified brick with curved top #6091

You can have the 1x6x3 1/3 arch with curved top (#6060) face in (top) or face out (bottom).

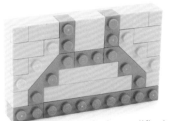

3x3 modified
facet brick #2462

1x6 modified plate #6583

1x3x2 arch #88292

4 x 2 1/2 x 1 2/3 round arch mudguard #50745

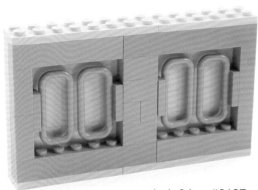

1x4x2 bar #6187

Tiles attached at angles on
1x1 bricks with stud on side (#87087)

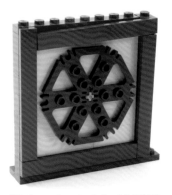

Water wheel plate #64566

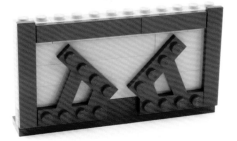

A-shape plate #15706

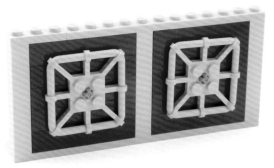

2x2 modified plate with
square frame #30094

4-blade propeller with
rounded ends #2479

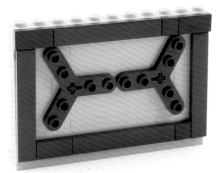

3-blade rotor #32125

Small bony leg #15064

Dinosaur tail #40379

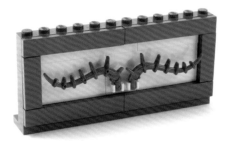

Plant vine #55236

How To: Timber Framing with Turntables

Turntable bases create a circular pattern that is reminiscent of timber framed woodwork. This effect works best when solid studs show through, so attach the turntable bases to plates.

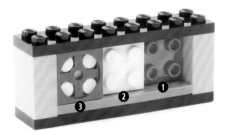

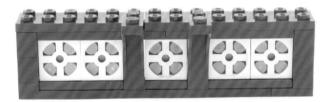

- ❶ 1x2 - 2x2 bracket #44728
- ❷ 2x2 plate #3022
- ❸ Turntable base #3680

Create simple contrasting frames using various dark-colored 1x bricks with white 1x2x5 bricks (#2454) or 1x2x2 bricks (#3245), which can also be set back on jumper plates.

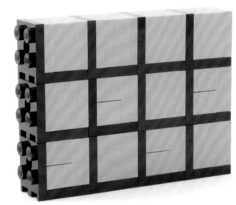

For a thinner frame,
use 2x2 - 2x2 brackets (#3956).

- ❶ 2x2 - 2x2 bracket #3956
- ❷ 2x2 plate #3022
- ❸ 2x2 brick #3003
- ❹ 1x1 brick with stud on side #87087
- ❺ 1x2 brick #3004

Simple Paneling

Panel pieces have defined edges that help break up a large section of wall. You can use this technique to add color or texture variations on an interior or exterior wall.

Large panels come in a variety of colors and sizes.

❶ 1x2x2 panel #87552
❷ 1x2x3 panel #87544
❸ 1x4x3 panel #60581
❹ 1x6x5 panel #59349

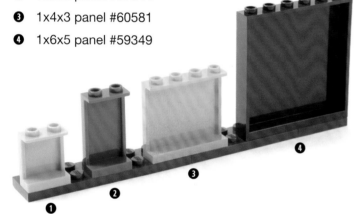

Combine different panels to create full-height walls.

❶ 1x2x2 panel #87552
❷ 1x4x3 panel #60581

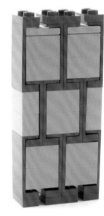

Line up multiple 1x2x2 panels (#87552) to create a shadow with the vertical edges.

Frame panels with 1x1 round bricks (#3062) or 1x1 bricks (#3005) in a contrasting color.

Panels can also be used sideways in an interlocking pattern that looks like masonry or grout.

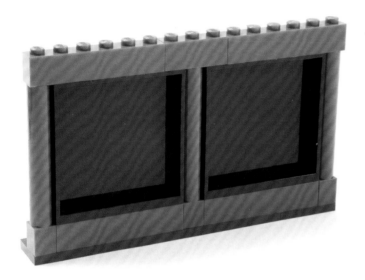

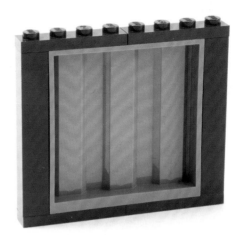

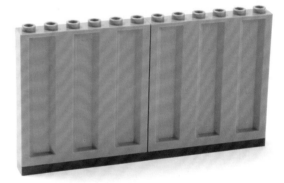

Framing a large panel in a contrasting color helps to add interest.

The 1x6x5 corrugated panel (#23405) has indentations that can act as narrow paneling.

2x6x6 log wall #30140

The 2x2 seat (#4079) has reinforced edges that create a similar effect. You can even flip the seats to face the other way for an interesting look, as the seat backs are slightly convex with rounded corners.

Paneling Using Containers

Use 2x2x2 containers (#61780) to give texture to exterior walls, especially those on the edge of a model that might otherwise seem too plain.

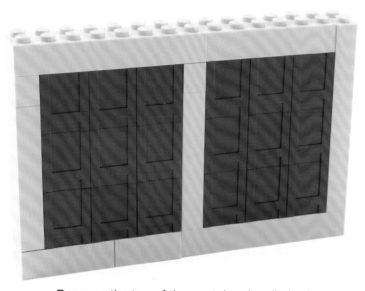

Because the top of the container has limited clutch power, you need to frame it with regular plates or bricks. Put an axle through the center of the container to give it extra strength.

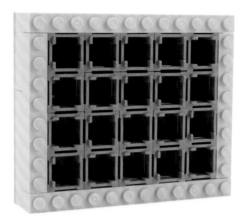

You can even use the top of container pieces for an interesting look.

The sides of the crate (#30150) have a slight relief pattern, which when stacked forms a subtle paneling effect. Crates should be framed because they have weak clutch power on top.

Layering 2x plates between each row of container pieces adds strength and additional texture.

Paneling Using Windows

Use window frames to create paneling and geometric patterns on walls. Fill the background using bricks in either the same or a contrasting color.

1x4x6 window frame
with 3 panes #57894

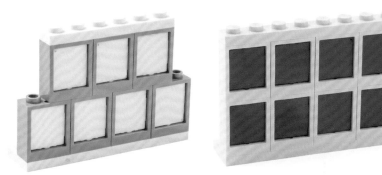

Fill frames with opaque, colored
1x2x2 window glass (#60601).

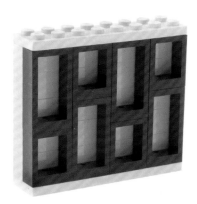

1x2x2 window #60592
1x2x3 window #60593

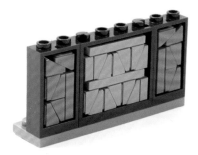

You can also fill windows with
1x1 cheese slopes (#54200), 1x2 tiles
(#3069), and 1x3 tiles (#63864)
to mimic masonry.

2x3x2 cupboards (#4532) and
doors (#4533)

Decorative Paneling

Use smooth tiles to create raised panels, or combine textured pieces like Scala plates and lift doors for a more ornate decorative effect.

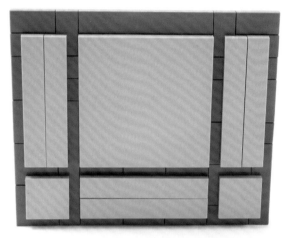

Create raised panels by attaching tiles to jumper plates to create half-stud recessed borders. The gaps expose the dark gray tiles underneath.

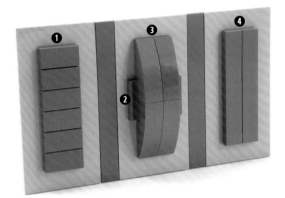

Use 4x8 modified plates with studs in center (#6576) with a variety of parts:

❶ 1x2 tile #3069
❷ 1x2 plate with rail #32028
❸ 1x3 curved slope #50950
❹ 1x6 tile #6636

How To: Recessed Panel Borders

Use panel pieces for a deeper recessed border.

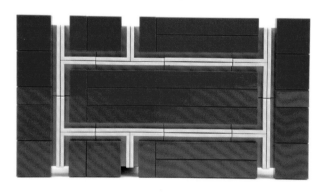

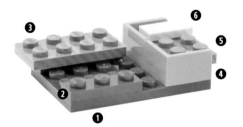

❶ 4x6 plate #3032
❷ 1x3 plate #3623
❸ 2x4 plate #3020
❹ 2x2x1 corner panel #91501
❺ 2x3 plate #3021
❻ 1x2 tile #3069

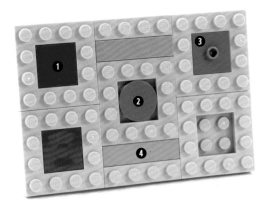

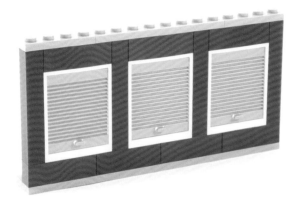

Using 4x4 plates with 2x2 cutout (#64799), create a natural frame that you can fill with different colors and textures.

❶ 2x2 tile #3068
❷ 2x2 round tile #4150
❸ 2x2 jumper plate #87580
❹ 1x4 tile #2431

Combine a 1x4x4 door frame (#6154) and a 1x4x4 lift door (#6155) for a panel with horizontal grooves.

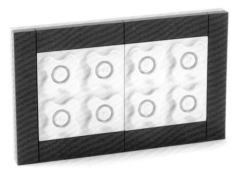

Use 1x1 round bricks (#3062) and 1x2 tiles (#3069) to give your panels some decorative framing.

The 4x4 Scala plate (#33062) has a quatrefoil shape that becomes a panel when framed by tiles. It also fits into the cutout of a 6x4 double inverted slope with 4x4 cutout (#30283).

The 6x3 hinge panel (#2440) has a beveled shape so that when used in a row, it creates a slightly concave wall.

Patterned Walls

Horizontal Stripes

Plates with rail create interesting striped shadows, even making plates of the same color appear darker.

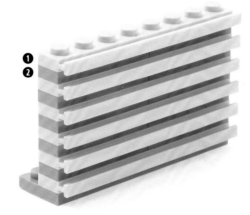

Go for a monochromatic look or use a contrasting color.

❶ 1x8 plate with rail #4510

❷ 1x8 plate #3460

Accentuate these shadows by using different colors between the layers. Here, dark tan, reddish brown, and dark brown plates create an ombré effect.

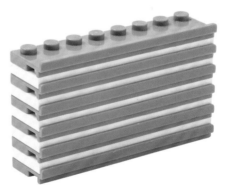

To create narrower stripes, alternate 2x8 plates with wide rail (#30586) and 2x8 plates (#3034).

Vertical Stripes

Combine plates (for structure) and the grooved edges of jumper plates and tiles to create a subtle vertical texture.

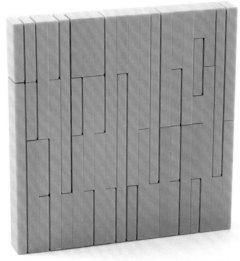

Use the newer style of jumper plates with groove for this technique.

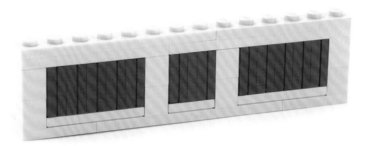

You can frame stacks of jumper plates (or jumper plates and standard plates) to make paneling. Attach the end of each stack to a brick with stud on side.

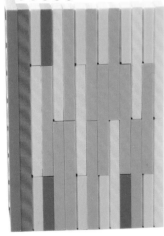

❶ 1x8 plate #3460
❷ 1x2 jumper plate with groove #15573
❸ 1x2 plate #3023
❹ 1x4 tile #2431
❺ 1x4 plate #3710

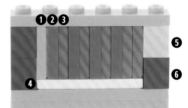

❶ 1x2 tile #3069
❷ 1x2 plate #3023
❸ 1x2 jumper plate #3794/#15573
❹ 1x4 tile #2431
❺ 1x1 brick with stud on side #87087
❻ 1x1 brick #3005

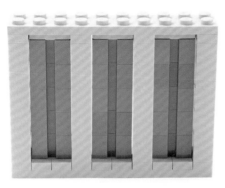

Stack 1x2 modified bricks with groove (#4216) and use jumper plates to set them back.

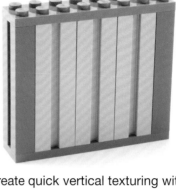

Create quick vertical texturing with 1x2x5 modified bricks with groove (#88393).

Use 1x8 plates with rail (#4510) to create a split wall.

Alternate the direction of 1x10 curved slopes (#85970) to create a contrasting pattern.

1x1 brick with handle #2921

1x4 Technic gear rack #3743

Geometric Patterns

Use small panels to create geometric patterns like those found in modern concrete buildings.

Use 1x4x1 panels (#30413) to make clean horizontal lines and shadows for a ribbed concrete-wall effect.

Place 1x2x1 panels (#4865) back to back in offset rows to create a pattern of horizontal (or vertical) ribs.

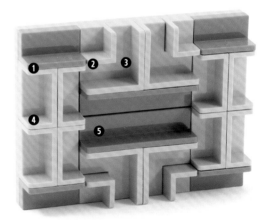

Create a pattern using a mix of panel shapes.

❶ 1x2x1 panel #4865
❷ 1x1x1 corner panel #6231
❸ 2x2x1 corner panel #91501
❹ 1x2x1 panel with 2 sides #23969
❺ 1x4x1 panel #30413

You can make a gridded pattern using 2x2x1 corner panels (#91501), which works well with or without the stud exposed.

Horizontal Tiles

Build a wall by using the sides of tiles to mimic flat stone slabs.

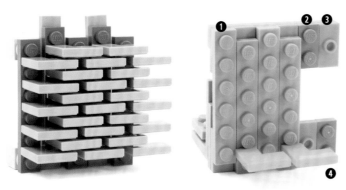

The L-shaped corner tiles are wedged *between* the studs of the plates. The vertical plates are offset by half a stud via a jumper plate.

❶ 1x6 plate #3666
❷ 1x2 plate #3023
❸ 1x2 jumper plate #3794/#15573
❹ 2x2 corner tile #14719

You can achieve a similar effect using hoses and plates with clips. The tiles attach to plates with clips so that each row is 2 plates thick.

❶ 1x2 Technic brick with axle hole #32064
❷ 3mm rigid hose #75
❸ 1x1 plate with horizontal clip #6019/#61252
❹ 1x1 tile #3070
❺ 1x2 tile #3069
❻ 1x2 plate with horizontal clips #60470

You can also "stack" tiles using 1x1 tiles with clip (#2555) or 1x2 plates with clip (#11476).

Patterned Tiles

There are endless possibilities for decorating walls with tiles.

2x2 corner plate #2420
1x1 quarter round tile #25269

1x1 quarter round tile #25269

2x2 tile #3068
1x1 round tile #98138
2x2 corner tile #14719

How To

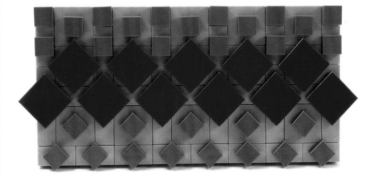

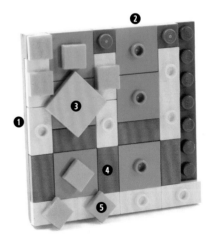

❶ 1x2 jumper plate #3794/#15573

❷ 2x2 jumper plate #87580

❸ 2x2 tile #3068

❹ 1x2 tile #3069

❺ 1x1 tile #3070

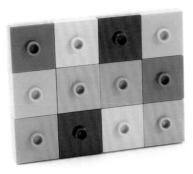

Use 2x2 jumper plates (#87580) in different colors for a modern, graphic design.

Create a polka-dot design with 2x2 round tiles (#14769) on a 1x1 Technic brick (#6541) with half pin (#4274) or a 1x1 brick with stud on side (#87087).

Mix 2x2 round tiles (#14769) and 1x1 round tiles (#98138) of different colors. The back wall is made of 1x2 Technic bricks (#3700) and half pins (#4274).

This monochromatic pattern uses 1x1 round tiles (#98138), 1x2 Technic bricks (#3700), and half pins (#4274).

Make a patterned stone wall by combining 1x1 round plates (#4073) with 1x2 Technic bricks (#3700) or using round plates with flower edge (#33291).

Checkerboard Walls

Use 1x1 bricks (#3005) in similar or contrasting colors to create a checkerboard pattern.

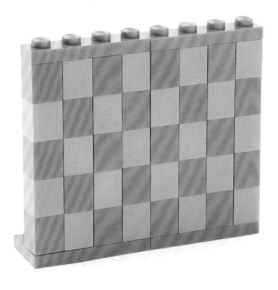

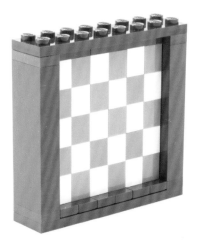

Frame a checkerboard pattern to turn it into a panel. Recess it by using 1x2 jumper plates (#3794/#15573).

How To: Houndstooth Walls

Headlight bricks have a setback and a lip on the front, which can create an interesting houndstooth pattern. The wall can be finished with tiles since the pattern has studs on all sides.

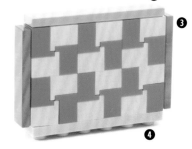

❶ 1x1 headlight brick #4070

❷ 1x6 tile #6636

❸ 1x4 tile #2431

❹ 1x6 plate #3666

Herringbone Walls

There are two types of 1x2 jumper plates: with a groove (#15573) and without (#3794). You can use either, but these patterns look best if you stick with one version.

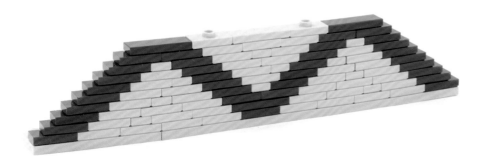

Use 1x2 jumper plates to create a V-shaped pattern. Fill in the rest of the wall with jumper plates and tiles of a different color.

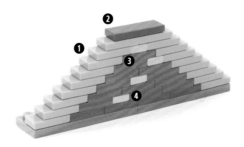

❶ 1x2 jumper plate with groove #15573

❷ 1x3 tile #63864

❸ 1x2 jumper plate without groove #3794

❹ 1x1 tile #3070

Stack jumper plates and then finish with tiles at the top to make a herringbone pattern that mimics intricate masonry, often used between the wood of timber-framed exteriors.

Use regular plates in contrasting colors to create a diamond or lozenge pattern.

Textured Walls

Texturing adds interest and shadows without changing colors or parts.

Place 1x2 triple slopes (#3048/#15571) together to make pyramids.

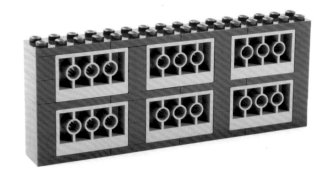

Frame 2x4x2 bricks with holes on sides (#6061) to display the pattern on the sides of the bricks.

Stack 2x3 modified plates with hole (#3176) to create a textured masonry wall.

How To: Woven Fence Texture

Stack Technic cams (#6575) in an offset pattern to create a rounded wall that mimics a woven fence.

These cams are stacked on axles to create a continuous line. The rows alternate in direction to create the overlapping pattern.

Greebling

Greebling is a technique that combines many little parts to create a mechanical-looking effect.

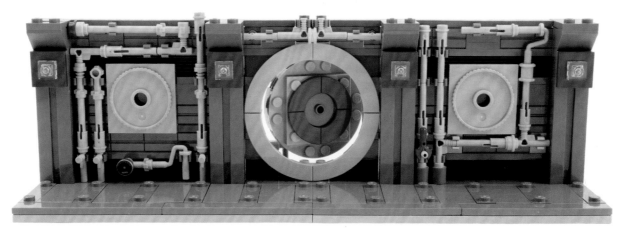

Which parts are used is not as important as the overall effect—you can choose whatever pieces would make interesting textures.

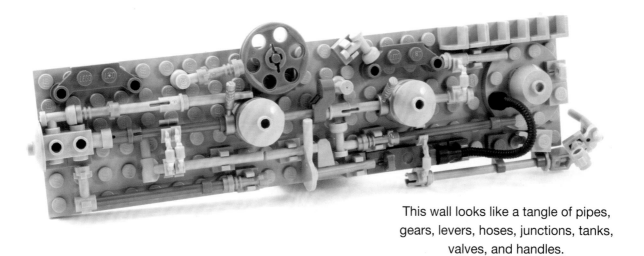

This wall looks like a tangle of pipes, gears, levers, hoses, junctions, tanks, valves, and handles.

Molding and Millwork

Horizontal Molding

Stacking elements can create interesting horizontal accents.

1x2 plate with rail #32028

1x14 brick with groove #4217

1x4 brick with groove #2653

2x3 modified plate
with hole #3176

Attach a flexible hose to
1x1 bricks with stud on side (#87087).

1x1 tile #3070

How To: Building Sideways

Create a zipper-like grooved pattern with plates
with rail by building sideways.

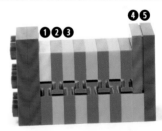

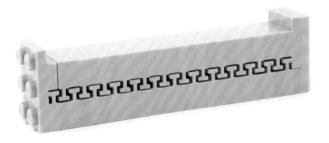

❶ 1x2 tile #3069

❷ 1x2 plate with rail #32028

❸ 1x2 plate #3023

❹ 2x2 jumper plate #87580

❺ 2x3 plate #3021

Vertical Molding

You can create vertical ornamentation with cones, goblets, telescopes, and more.

Set telescopes (#64644)
on studs.

Or fit telescopes into clips
for added detail.

Handle with side studs #92690

Goblets (#2343) can fit side by side
in a variety of interesting patterns.

Add 1x1 round plates (#4073)
for more detail.

Lightsaber hilt #64567

Combine the Technic half pin
with bar extension (#61184)
and 1x1 cone (#4589).

Cricket bat (by BrickArms)

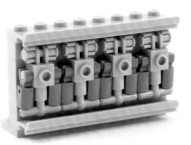

Insert the pneumatic hose T (#4697)
into a mechanical torso (#24078) and
fit into a bar holder with clip (#11090).

Panel Accents

Create interesting geometric patterns with panels, grills, and other textured pieces.

Create repeating pockets of space using 1x1x1 corner panels (#6231).

1x1 headlight brick #4070

1x2 grill plate #2412

1x4 Technic gear rack #3743

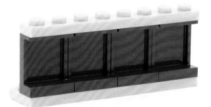

1x2x2 panel #87552

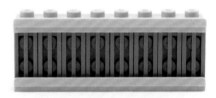

1x2 grill plate #2412

1x2x2 2/3 sloping vehicle grille #50946
1x2 modified brick with groove #4216

1x2x2 plane window #2377

2x4 hinge plate #2873
1x2 hinge plate with finger on side #44567

Egg-and-Dart Molding

Combine sockets and towballs to re-create the classical egg-and-dart ornamentation found in Greek and Roman architecture.

1x2 modified plate with socket on end #14418

1x2 modified plate with socket on side #14704

❶ 1x2 modified plate with socket on end #14418

❷ Technic axle towball #2736

❸ 2x8 plate with wide rail #30586

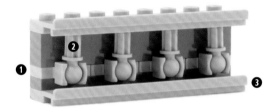

❶ 1x2 modified plate with socket on side #14704

❷ Technic axle towball #2736

❸ 2x8 plate with wide rail #30586

1L bar with towball #22484

❶ 2x2 plate with 1 pin hole #2444
(or 2 pin holes #2817)

❷ Technic axle towball #2736

Modified Plate with Tooth

You can also re-create the egg-and-dart look with the 1x1 modified plate with horizontal tooth (#49668). This piece also comes in a version at a right angle (#15070), which has a similar profile but without the exposed stud.

Line them up for a simple take on egg-and-dart molding.

Attach 1x1 cheese slopes (#54200) to the exposed studs on the tooth.

Attach 1x1 round tiles (#98138) to the exposed studs on the tooth.

Align two rows of plates to make a diamond pattern.

Add plates with rail above and below your row of plates with tooth to add more depth.

Layer different pieces to gradually increase the depth of your molding.

Circular and Rosette Molding

Plates, tiles, gears, and shields provide lots of options for creating circular molding and wall accents.

Line up 1x1 round plates with swirled top (#15470) to mimic classical spiral motifs.

1x1 round tile #98138
1x1 round plate with swirled top #15470

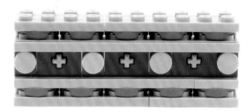

1x2 Technic brick with axle hole #32064

1x1 round plate #4073

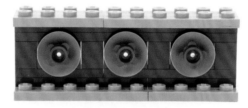

2x2 dish #4740
1x1 round plate with flower edge #33291

12-tooth gear #6589

2x2 round tile with SW pattern #4150pb086

Ovoid shield with SW pattern #2586px15

Scorpion shield #48494pb05

Fence Patterns

Fences are a great way to add interest to your models, especially when using contrasting colors.

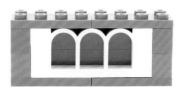

1x4x1 fence #3633
1x1 cone #4589

1x4x2 fence #3185

Line up 1x2 plates with ladder (#4175) for a more modern take on this effect.

1x6x2 fence #30077

1x4x2 fence #30055/#15332

Alternate 1x2 plates with angled handles (#92692) to create a fence pattern.

Frame a 1x4x2 ornamental fence (#19121) with other pieces, like telescopes or modified bricks.

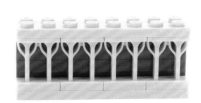

AltBricks 1x2x2 fence

Slopes and Modified Bricks

You can arrange slopes and modified bricks to add textured accents. Include plates between layers to add definition.

2x1x1 slope #60481

1x1 cheese slope #54200

4x1 double curved slope #93273

1x3 double inverted slope #2341

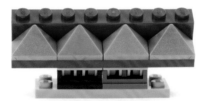

1x2 triple slope #3048/#15571

2x4 mudguard with flared wings #41854
2x2 curved slope
with 3 side ports #44675

1x2x2/3 brick with wing end #47458

2x3x2/3 brick with
wing end #47456

1x2 curved slope #11477
2x2 modified brick
with sloped end #47457

Corbels

Corbels are support structures for roofs, windows, upper levels, and even parapets. They can be functional or decorative.

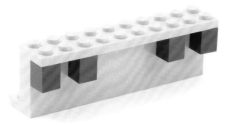

1x1 brick #3005

1x2 curved slope #11477

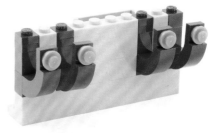

1x3x2 arch with curved top #6005

1x2x1 1/3 modified brick
with curved top #6091
1x4x1 1/3 modified brick
with curved top #6191

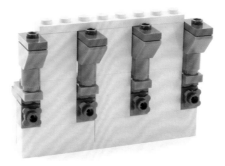

1x2 inverted slope #3665

1x5x4 arch #2339
1x3x3 arch #13965

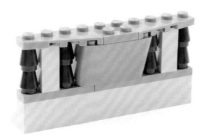

2x4x2 inverted windscreen #4284

1 1/2x6x1 arch mudguard #62361
2x2 curved slope #15068

1x3x3 arch #13965

Microfigs and Minifigs

You can use microfigures and minifigures to mimic the look of sculptures in a pediment—or take them apart and use their legs and torsos as structural elements!

The microfig (#85863) comes in a wide variety of colors. Alternate two contrasting colors to create a simple pattern.

Offset microfigures using jumper plates.

Here, microfigs with helmets (#94162) stand on jumper plates while the 1x2x3 panels (#2362) behind them add interesting vertical ridges.

Minifigure legs (#970c00) can be placed upright or bent at the hips for a slight angle.

How To: Short Legs

Short legs (#41879) need bricks on top for the hips to fit into. Use bricks with studs to add a front-facing detail.

❶ 1x4 brick with 4 studs on side #30414

❷ Short legs #41879

❸ 1x8 plate with rail #4510

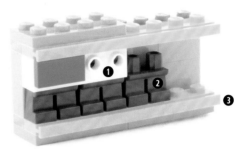

Skeleton leg #6266

Space out skeleton legs with bars on top.

Skeleton leg with black boot #93062

Bent skeleton arm #93609

A minifig head (#3626) is wider than a stud, so space them out using jumper plates.

Martian leg #x118

Droids and Robots

Star Wars droids and robots have unique angles and shapes that come in handy for creating architectural details.

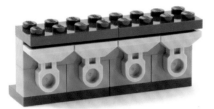

Short droid leg #17486

Droid leg #30362

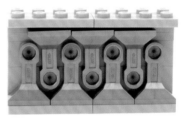

Droid leg #30362

Droid head #30378

Battle droid legs #30376

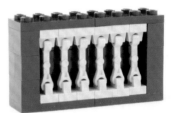

Robot arm straight #59230

How To: Robot Arms

Robot arms create a nice angle that can be framed by 2x1x2 slopes. The arms are connected with an axle through the base.

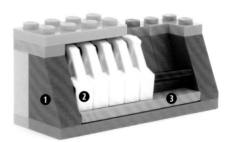

❶ 2x1x2 slope #60481

❷ Mechanical arm #53989/#98313

❸ 1x6 tile #6636

Fists and Claws

Bionicle fists and claw pieces can also be used as wall decorations to great effect.

Use axles to line up Bionicle fists (#93575).

Clip Bionicle fists onto the 2x2 brick with ball and axle hole (#57909).

Bionicle fists can also be connected with Technic axle pins (#3749).

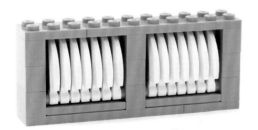

Claw with clip #16770

Bladed claw #10187

BrickForge fighting claw

Animals

You can use unusual pieces like animal elements to re-create motifs on a cornice or pediment.

Antler #11437

Cat tail #15429

Dragon plume #x47

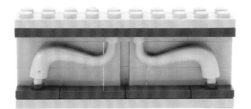

Elephant tail/trunk #43892

Ornamental fish #x59
Bionicle knee cover #47299

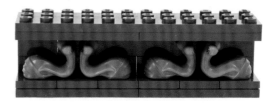

SW Ithorian head #16475

Ponytail #22411

Snake #98136

Plants

Mimic the look of floral and foliage decorations not only with actual plant pieces but also with other small decorative elements.

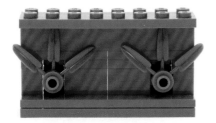

Bamboo plant #30176

Feathered plume #6029

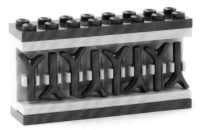

Carrot top #33183

Plant curved stem #28870

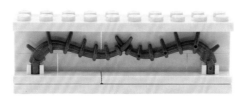

Plant vine #55236

Croissants (#33125) mimic
ornamental palmettes.

1x1 round plate
with flower edge #33291

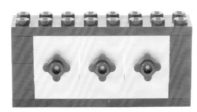

1x1 round plate
with flower edge #33291

1x1 round brick
with flower edge #33286

Tools and Sundry Items

LEGO tools can create a mechanical and futuristic look, but with a little creativity, tools can also mimic traditional architectural ornamentation and framing.

Ornate key #19118

Wheel wrench #11402d

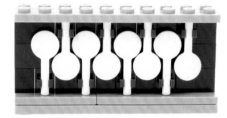

Signal paddle #3900

Phone #6190

Tap #4599

Ice skates #93555

Binoculars #30162

1x3 bar with clip and stud #4735

Toy winder key #98375

Ice cream cone #11610

Space gun/torch #3959/#86208

Axe #3835

Airtanks #3838

Quadruple axle connector #11272

Small lever base #4592

Nozzle #60849

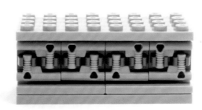

Nozzle #60849

Pneumatic hose T #4697

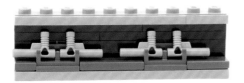

Handcuffs #61482

Pantograph shoe #2922

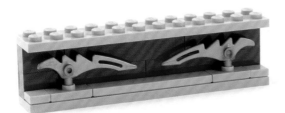

Weapon crescent blade #98141

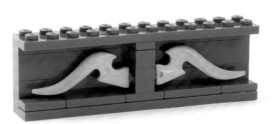

Flame #18395

5-link chain #92338

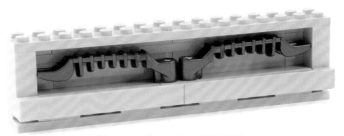

Thornax launcher #64275

Hinges, Clips, and Handles

Because there are many hinge, clip, and handle parts, you can easily exchange one for another to create subtle differences in style.

Sandwich 3x4 hinge plates (#44570) between 2x8 plates with rail (#4510).

1x2 hinge brick locking with fingers #30386 (in alternating directions)

Use 1x2 plates with clip on top (#92280) to hold 4L bars (#30374).

1x2 plate with handle on side #2540/#48336

Attach bar holders with clip (#11090) to 1x2 plates with handle on side (#48336).

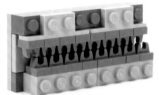

1x1 tile with clip #2555

1x1 tile with clip #2555

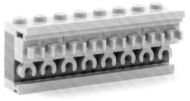

Combine 1x1 plates with vertical clip (#4085) with 1x1 tiles with clip (#15712).

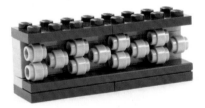

Stagger 1x1 plates with ring (#4081).

1x1 brick with handle #2921

Stagger 1x4 plates with arm down (#30043) and 1x2 plates with arm up (#4623/#88072).

1x2 plate with pin hole on bottom #18677

Simple Windows

Basic Windows

The simplest windows are the premade window pieces, but they come in a variety of sizes and styles, allowing for easy customization.

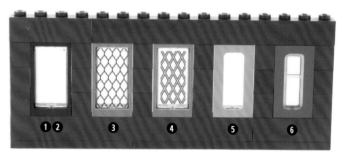

Basic windows come in a number of styles, and they can each be fitted with their matching glass piece.

❶ 1x2x2 window #60592

❷ 1x2x2 window glass #60601

❸ 1x2x2 printed glass from set #41174

❹ 1x2x2 castle window #90195

❺ 1x2x2 plane window #2377

❻ 1x4x2 plane window #4863

❼ 1x2x2 plane window glass #4862

Custom printed glass and stickers add interest to basic windows. Special train window glass even re-creates a divided pane.

❶ 1x2x3 window #60593

❷ 1x2x3 window glass #60602

❸ 1x2x3 custom printed glass (PromoTec)

❹ 1x2x3 sticker from set #70413

❺ 1x2x3 train window #4035

❻ 1x2x3 train window glass #4036

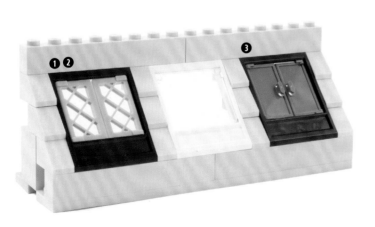

Angled window frames fit standard window panes, window glass, and solid shutters.

❶ 4x4x3 roof window with bottom panel #60806

❷ 1x2x3 window pane lattice with tabs #60607

❸ 1x2x3 door with handle #60614

Window Panes

Window panes without tabs can swing freely, whereas window panes with tabs have enough friction that they will stay where you position them. Train windows fit a single glass pane.

❶ 1x4x3 window #60594

❷ 1x2x3 window pane lattice #2529

❸ 1x2x3 window pane lattice with tabs #60607

❹ 1x4x3 window glass #3855

❺ 2x4x3 window #60598

❻ 1x2x3 window pane #3854

❼ 1x2x3 window pane with tabs #60608

❽ 1x4x3 bar window #62113

❾ 2x4x3 window #4132

❿ 2x4x3 window pane #4133

⓫ 1x4x3 train window #4033/#6556

⓬ 1x4x3 window glass #3855

⓭ 1x4x3 train window glass #4034

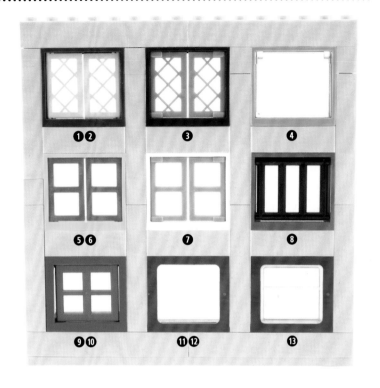

Shutters

Add colorful detail to your windows using shutters. Some have built-in clip handles while others fit into tabs on window frames.

❶ 1x2x3 shutter with hinges and handle #60800

❷ 1x1x3 brick with 2 clips #60583

❸ 1x4x3 window #60594

❹ 1x2x3 window pane with tabs #60608

❺ 1x2x3 window pane lattice #2529

❻ 1x2x3 shutter #3856

❼ 1x4x3 window #3853

❽ 1x2x3 window pane #3854

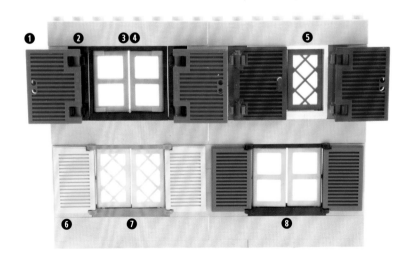

Large Windows

Use large window pieces with printed glass, stickers, or divided panels to create screen doors or French windows.

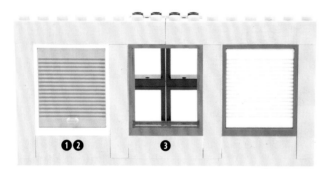

❶❷   **❸**

- ❶ 1x4x4 lift door frame #6154
- ❷ 1x4x4 lift door #6155
- ❸ 1x2x2 window #60592

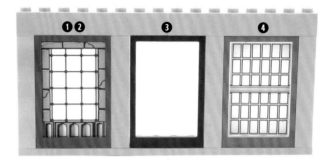

❶❷   **❸**   **❹**

- ❶ 1x4x5 window #2493
- ❷ 1x4x5 printed glass (from set #4719/#4756)
- ❸ 1x4x5 window glass #2494
- ❹ 1x4x5 printed glass (from set #4856)

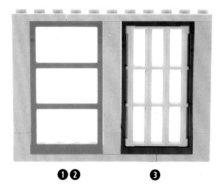

❶❷   **❸**

- ❶ 1x4x6 door frame #30179/#60596
- ❷ 1x4x6 window frame with 3 panes #6160
- ❸ 1x4x6 bar with end protrusions #92589

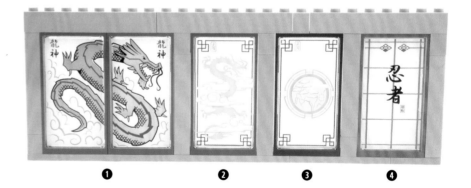

❶   **❷**   **❸**   **❹**

- ❶ 1x4x6 printed glass (from set #2507)
- ❷ 1x4x6 printed glass (from set #70505)
- ❸ 1x4x6 printed glass (from set #70751)
- ❹ 1x4x6 printed glass (from set #2520)

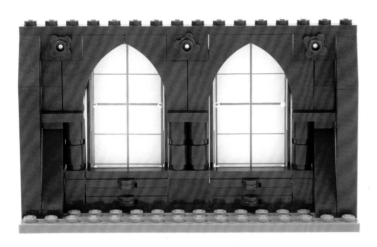

Combine large windows with arches
to create a more interesting silhouette.

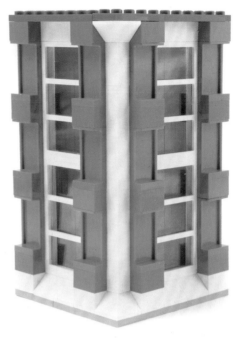

Divided panes work well in modern facades.

Wall Panel Windows

These large wall panel pieces have built-in window cutouts.

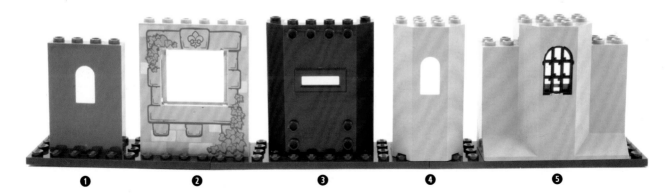

① **②** **③** **④** **⑤**

① 1x4x5 panel with window #60808

② 1x6x6 with window #15627

③ 2x6x6 panel with window slot #22387

④ 3x4x6 turret wall panel with window #30246

⑤ 3x8x6 panel with window #48490
     1x2x2 2/3 pane with twisted bar and rounded top #30045

Plate-Glass Windows

Transparent panels and bricks make for great frameless windows!

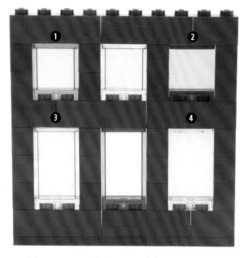

Newer panels have side supports, and their reinforced edges create a subtle line that looks like a plate-glass window.

❶ 1x2x2 panel with side supports #87552

❷ 1x2x2 panel #4864

❸ 1x2x3 panel with side supports #87544

❹ 1x2x3 panel #2362

❶ 1x6x3 windscreen #64453

❷ 1x6x5 panel #59349

❸ 1x6x5 sticker from set #75919

❹ 1x6x5 sticker from set #10222

1x4x3 panel #60581

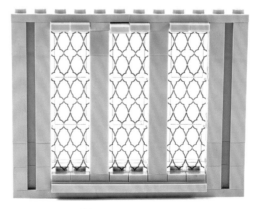

Use custom printing or stickers to make panels look like floor-to-ceiling windows.

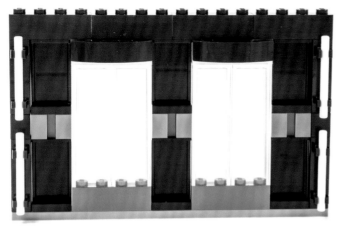

The edges of the transparent 1x2x5 bricks (#46212) give this window a tall profile.

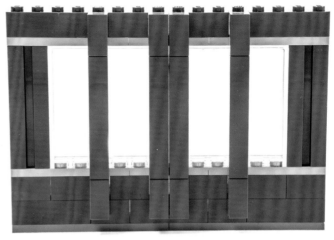

Subdivide large panels by layering tiles in front.

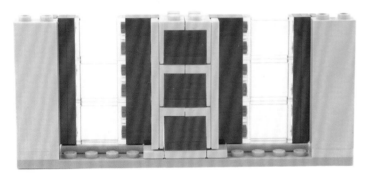

Mount panels sideways to create tall frameless windows.

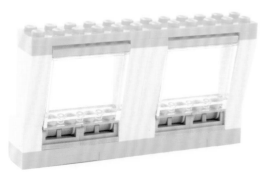

Use hinge bricks to tilt window panels so that they follow the shape of the inverted slope frame.

Stack panels to create a double-hung window.

Sunrooms and Greenhouses

Use transparent pieces to build walls and roofs and create your own sunrooms and greenhouses.

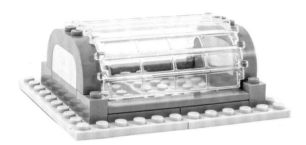

Transparent garage roller door sections (#4218) can be either laid flat or bent around an arch piece to create a curved skylight.

Create a curved sunroom using transparent 4x4x6 quarter panels (#46361).

Top off your structure with garage roller door sections (#4218) to create an all-glass roof.

Combine standard windows with slopes to create angled skylights.

Custom Windows

Mullions and Muntins

Combine window frames in different ways to create vertical and horizontal window divisions, which are called mullions and muntins, respectively.

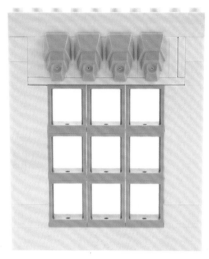

Basic frames can be arranged to create divided panes.

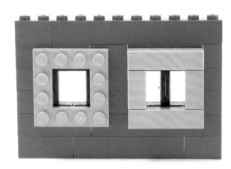

Stagger frames behind even small openings to create a mullion.

Stack two windows to create mullions (left) or offset four windows to create muntins (right).

The 1x2 plate with rail (#32028) gives a subtle divider.

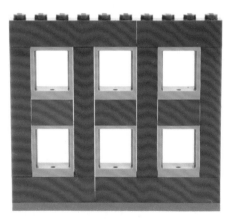

Bricks make for thick and colorful dividers between frames.

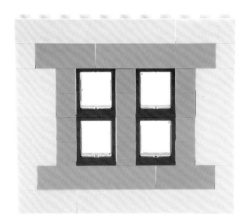

A brick border in a contrasting color emphasizes the top and bottom.

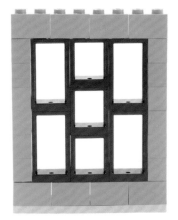

Mix window sizes and
stagger the frames.

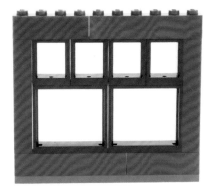

Mix smaller frames
with larger ones.

Create a more modern look
with asymmetric staggering
and a textured frame.

Stagger differently sized
frames with bricks.

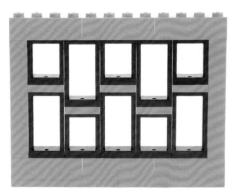

Stagger frames with plates for a
slightly subtler offset.

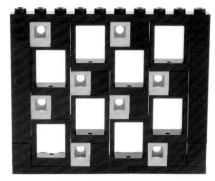

Add color-block emphasis with
1x1 headlight bricks (#4070).

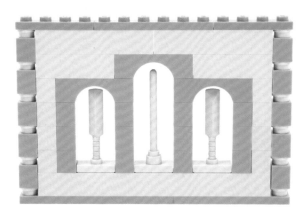

Create decorative mullions
with interesting parts like
cricket bats (by BrickArms)
and pitchforks (#95345).

Sideways Window Mounts

Mount windows sideways for additional size and pattern options.

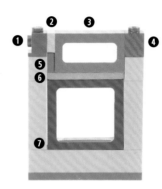

① 1x1 headlight brick #4070
② 1x1 plate #3024
③ 1x2x3 train window #4035
④ 1x1 brick with stud on side #87087
⑤ 1x1 tile #3070
⑥ 1x4 tile #2431
⑦ 1x4x3 train window #4033

Brick-Built Mullions

Create mullions without window panes by separating tiles with plates or bricks.

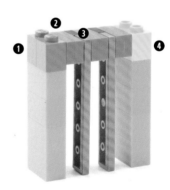

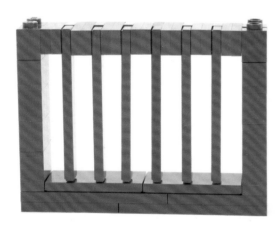

① 1x1 brick with stud on side #87087
② 1x2 plate #3023
③ 1x6 tile #6636
④ 1x2 Technic brick with 2 holes #32000

Panel Windows

Turn panels sideways to create open windows. Some panels have a thinner profile than others.

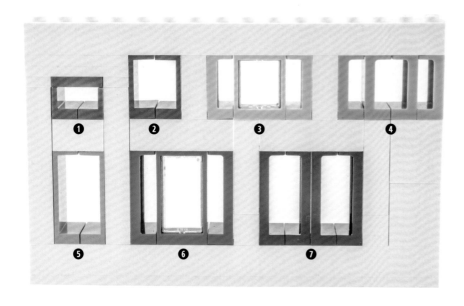

1. 1x2 plate #3023
   1x2x1 panel #4865
2. 1x2x2 panel #4864
3. 1x2x2 panel with side supports #87552
   1x2x2 window #60592
4. 1x2x2 panel with side supports #87552
5. 1x2x3 panel #2362
6. 1x2x3 panel with side supports #87544
   1x2x3 window #60593
7. 1x2x3 panel with side supports #87544

The windows shown on the left are made from panels without side supports, so their edge profile is narrower than those of the panel windows shown on the right.

Custom Window Shapes

You can use slopes, arches, and other brick pieces to create custom geometric window openings.

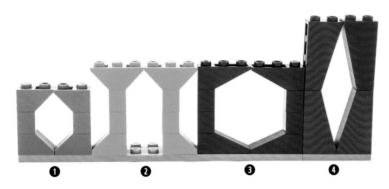

Pair straight or curved slopes with their inverted counterparts to create symmetrical geometric openings.

❶ 1x2 inverted slope #3665
1x2 slope #3040

❷ 1x3 double inverted slope #2341
1x2 slope #3040

❸ 1x3 inverted slope #4287
1x3 slope #4286

❹ 1x2x3 inverted slope #2449
1x2x3 slope #4460

❺ 1x2 inverted curved slope #24201
1x2 curved slope #11477

❻ 1x4 inverted curved slope #13547
1x4 curved slope #61678

❼ 1x6 inverted curved slope #42023
1x6 curved slope #42022

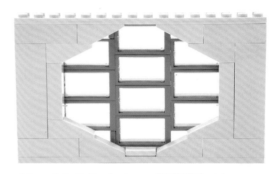

Mount 1x2x3 windows (#60593) sideways to make landscape-oriented panes framed in an octagonal opening.

Use 1x4 curved slopes (#61678) and 1x4 inverted curved slopes (#13547) to frame the top and bottom edges of a window.

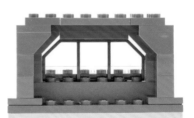

Repurpose a train element (1x6 modified plate with train wagon end #6583) to make a horizontal or vertical window.

Round Windows

Create a round window by combining an arch with either another arch or two inverted arches.

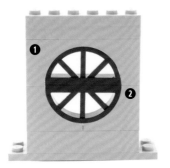

This window fits only with arches with thin tops but can be oriented in different ways.

❶ 1x6x2 arch #12939

❷ 1x4x1 2/3 window with rounded top #20309

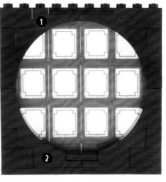

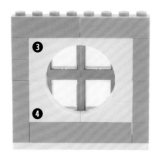

Create divided panels for round windows by layering basic window frames behind them.

❶ 1x5x4 arch #2339

❷ 1x5x4 inverted arch #30099

❸ 1x6x2 arch #3307/#12939/ #15254

❹ 1x3x2 inverted arch #18653

Oval Windows

You can frame an oval opening using two arches.

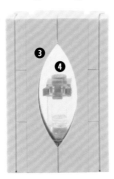

❶ 1x6 arch #3455

❷ Printed oval shield (from set #75080)

❸ Oval shield #92747

❹ 1x1 plate with horizontal clip #6019

Decorative Windows

Here are some simple ways to create unique brick-built window openings.

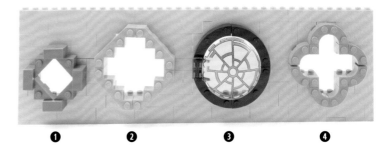

❶ 3x3 modified facet brick #2462

❷ 4x4 modified facet brick #14413

❸ 4x4 macaroni brick #48092

❹ 2x2 macaroni brick #3063

Bracket Windows

Combine two or more brackets to build small rectangular windows.

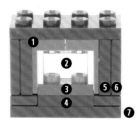

- ❶ 1x2 - 2x2 bracket #44728
- ❷ 1x2 brick without tube #3065
- ❸ 1x2 plate #3023
- ❹ 2x2 plate #3022
- ❺ 1x2 tile #3069
- ❻ 2x2 tile #3068
- ❼ 2x4 plate #3020

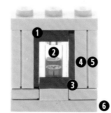

- ❶ 1x2 - 2x2 bracket #44728
- ❷ 1x1 brick #3005
- ❸ 1x2 - 2x2 inverted bracket #99207
- ❹ 1x2 plate #3023
- ❺ 1x2 tile #3069
- ❻ 1x3 plate #3623

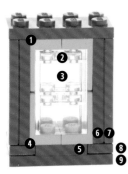

- ❶ 1x2 - 2x2 bracket #44728
- ❷ 1x2 plate #3023
- ❸ 1x2 brick without tube #3065
- ❹ 1x2 - 2x2 inverted bracket #99207
- ❺ 2x2 plate #3022
- ❻ 2x4 plate #3020
- ❼ 2x4 tile #87079
- ❽ 1x2 tile #3069
- ❾ 2x4 plate #3020

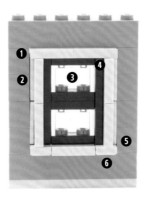

- ❶ 1x2 plate with rail #32028
- ❷ 1x2 - 2x2 bracket #44728
- ❸ 1x2 brick without tube #3065
- ❹ 1x4 tile #2431
- ❺ 1x1 brick with stud on side #87087
- ❻ 1x2 jumper plate #3794/#15573

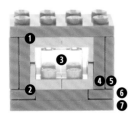

- ❶ 1x2 - 1x2 bracket #99781
- ❷ 1x2 - 1x2 inverted bracket #99780
- ❸ 1x2 brick without tube #3065
- ❹ 2x2 plate #3022
- ❺ 2x2 tile #3068
- ❻ 1x2 tile #3069
- ❼ 2x4 plate #3020

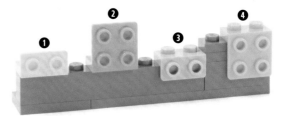

- ❶ 1x2 - 1x2 inverted bracket #99780
- ❷ 1x2 - 2x2 inverted bracket #99207
- ❸ 1x2 - 1x2 bracket #99781
- ❹ 1x2 - 2x2 bracket #44728

Microscale Windows

Stacking transparent plates and bricks creates frameless windows that are particularly useful in microscale buildings.

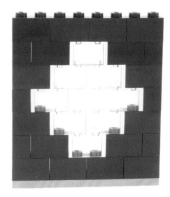

You can use the subtle lines created by the edges and studs as window pane divisions.

Stacked plates make even smaller subdivisions than bricks and create the look of leaded glass panes.

How To

Clear plates and bricks create minimalist windows.

❶ 1x1 brick #3005

❷ 1x1 plate #3024

❸ 1x1 cheese slope #54200

❹ 1x2 brick without tube #3065

❺ 1x2x1 panel #4865

❻ 1x2 plate #3023

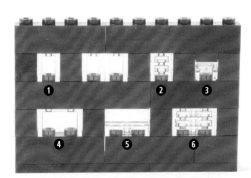

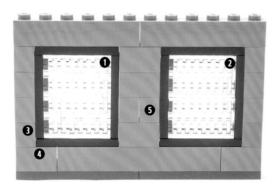

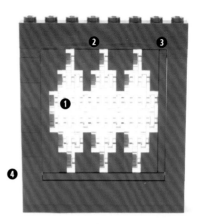

❶ 1x2 plate #3023   ❹ 1x4 tile #2431

❷ 1x1 plate #3024   ❺ 1x1 brick with stud
                               on side #87087

❸ 1x4 plate #3710

❶ 1x2 plate #3023   ❸ 1x6 tile #6636

❷ 1x1 plate #3024   ❹ 1x1 brick with stud
                               on side #87087

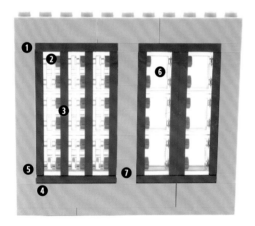

Unlike regular bricks, transparent bricks have
no tube on the bottom for a stud.

❶ 1x4 plate #3710   ❺ 1x6 tile #6636

❷ 1x2 plate #3023   ❻ 1x2 brick without tube #3065

❸ 1x6 plate #3666   ❼ 1x1 brick with studs on 2 sides
                               #47905

❹ 1x4 tile #2431

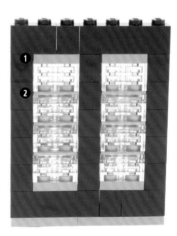

Use hinge brick tops to create super-thin
muntins that pair well with microscale windows.

❶ 1x2 plate #3023

❷ 1x2 hinge brick top #3938

Tiny Windows

The holes in headlight and Technic bricks can be used as tiny windows for your microscale structures.

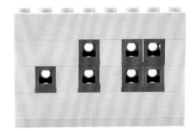

You can also use the backs of 1x1 headlight bricks (#4070) to create windows.

Fit Technic bricks with transparent plates and tiles to give them the look of glass.

How To

Technic bricks have holes for pins and axles, but these holes also work well as tiny windows.

❶ 1x1 Technic brick #6541

❷ 1x2 Technic brick with 1 hole #3700

❸ 1x2 Technic brick with 2 holes #32000

❹ 1x2 Technic brick with axle hole #32064

❺ 1x2 Technic pin connector plate #32530

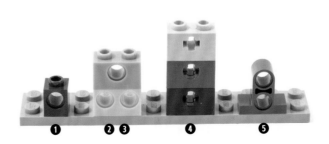

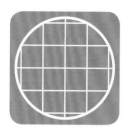

Bay Windows

Bay windows project out from the surrounding walls. They commonly have a flat front and two angled sides.

The 3x8x6 bay window (#30185) is a ready-made bay window with transparent glass glued into the frame.

The bay window piece fits perfectly on the 3x3 wedge brick (#30505).

Stack 2x6x2 train front windows (#17454) for a quick and easy bay window.

You can also build bay windows where the windows span the entire length of the walls.

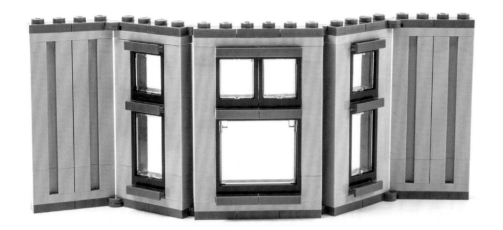

You can vary the angle of the side windows by using hinge plates to connect the walls.

Or you can use wedge plates for a fixed angle. This gives your window a very subtle bay shape.

A small window in the center of each wall segment allows for wall detailing.

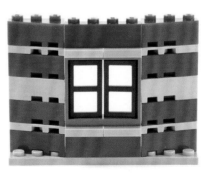

Use 2x3 wedge bricks (#6564/#6565) and plates (#43723/#43722) to make a small bay window.

Bow Windows

Bow windows are bay windows that have more than three sides and may even form a more curved shape.

This bow window is made completely out of 1x4x3 windows (#60594).

This bow window is made completely out of transparent 1x2x5 bricks (#2454).

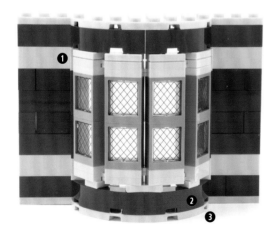

❶ 1x4 hinge plate #2429 with #2430

❷ 4x4 macaroni brick #48092

❸ 4x8 round plate #22888

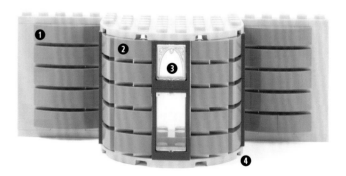

❶ 1x4 double curved slope #93273

❷ 1x2 curved slope #11477

❸ 1x2x2 printed glass (from set #41174)

❹ 4x8 round plate #22888

1x2 plate #3023

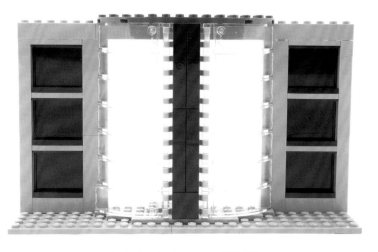

6x2x2 windscreen #92474

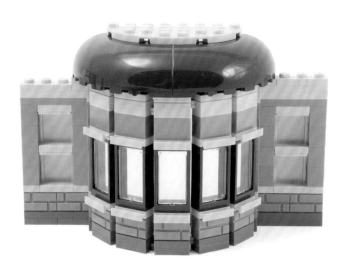

6x6x2 round corner brick #87559

2x4x5 half cylinder bricks #85941

Box Windows

Box windows are bay windows whose sides form a right angle.

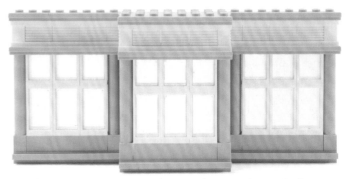

Use columns and cornices to frame a box window.

You can mix different window framing and roof treatments.

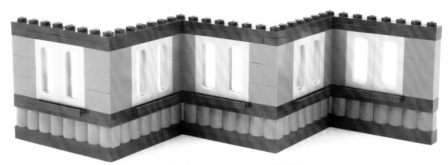

1x2x3 train window #4035

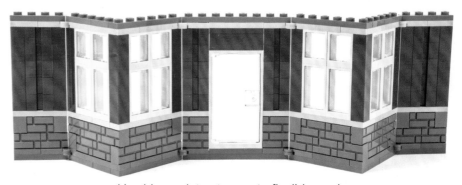

Use hinge plates to create flexible angles or corner plates for fixed angles.

Use a shallow popout to emphasize a window.

2x3 tile with 2 clips #30350

Kitchen box window

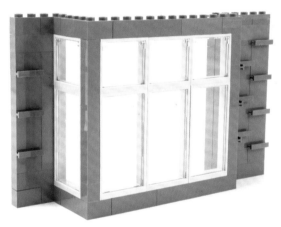

Box windows don't have to be symmetrical!

Contrasting panels and bricks

Pop out a window by 1 or 2 studs.

Recessed and Raised Windows

Regardless of how you build your window, how it sits in the wall is important to its overall look.

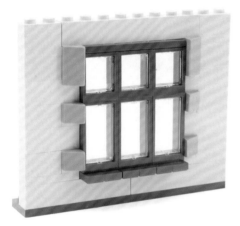

Use 1x2 jumper plates (#3794/#15573) to offset windows by half a stud.

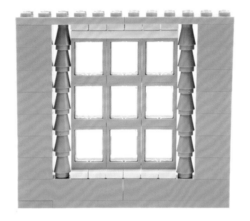

Or use jumper plates to inset windows by half a stud.

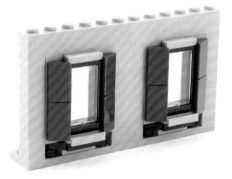

You can also use 1x4 offset plates (#4590) for a half-stud offset.

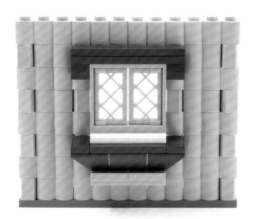

Offset a window so it can sit on a windowsill.

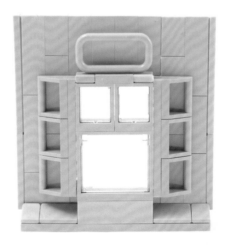

This window is offset one stud forward and framed with 1x2 tiles with handle (#2432).

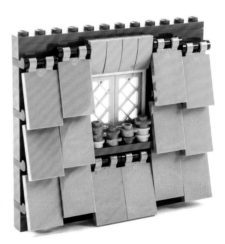

Set back a window by one stud to create a decorative window box.

Ornamental Windows

Romanesque Windows

Set arched windows flush with the wall, or create a recessed romanesque window by setting rectangular windows behind an arch.

Top 1x2x2 2/3 windows with rounded top (#30044) with arched bricks.

❶ 1x4x2 arch #6182

❷ 1x4 arch #3659

❸ 1x6x2 arch #3307/#12939/#15254

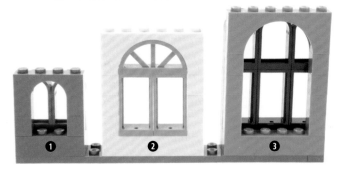

Set window frames behind arched bricks or mix windows with round tops with basic window frames.

❶ 1x2x2 2/3 window with rounded top #30044
1x4x2 arch #6182

❷ 1x4x1 2/3 window with rounded top #20309
1x2x3 window #60593
1x6x2 arch #3307/#12939/#15254

❸ 1x2x2 2/3 window with rounded top #30044
1x2x3 window #60593
1x6x2 arch #3307/#12939/#15254

These windows are set back by a full stud behind the arches and create an interesting muntin-mullion pattern.

Contrasting colors and
layered framing create a
nice double arch.

Use 2x2 macaroni tiles (#27925)
to create a rounded trim that mimics
the shape of the arched window.

Cap a square opening with a
1x6 raised arch (#92950).

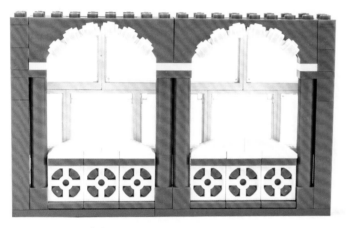

Add decorative elements like
1x1 plates with ring (#4081).

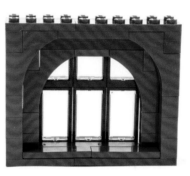

The double arch gives this large-scale divided
window a more ornate look.

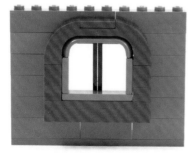

The 4x3x1 mudguard (#28326) fits neatly under a
pair of 1x3x2 arches with curved top (#6005).

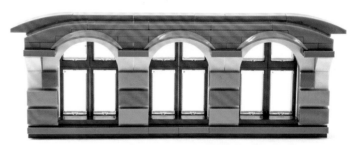

Frame multiple windows with the 1 1/2x6x1 arch
mudguard (#62361) for a unified look.

Gothic Windows

Half-arches can be used to make the pointed arches that are characteristic of gothic architecture.

Use the 1x3x2 inverted arch (#18653) to create a teardrop window.

This lancet window also uses half-arches as its base.

Filling in the space surrounding the window with slopes creates the look of masonry.

1x3x3 arch #13965

1x3x2 arch with curved top #6005

1x2 triple slope #3048

1x3x2 arch #88292

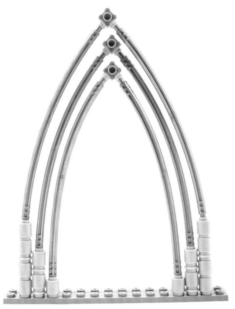

A 16L soft axle hose (#32202) creates a triple arch.

Fit 1x1 round bricks (#3062) on a 3mm hose (#75), which then fits into the end of a #5 angled axle connector (#32015) at the top. Control the shape of the arch with the length of the hose.

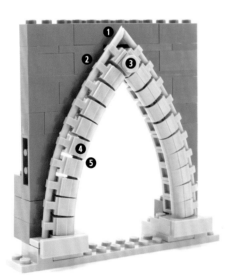

❶ 3mm rigid hose #75

❷ 1x2 plate with clip on top #92280

❸ 1x1 brick with stud on 2 adjacent sides #26604

❹ 1x2 plate with pin hole on bottom #18677

❺ 11L soft axle hose #32199 (inside pin holes)

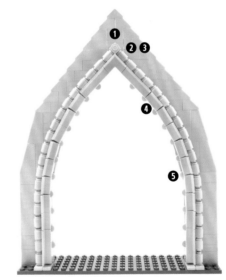

❶ 1x1 brick with stud on 2 adjacent sides #26604

❷ 1x1 round brick #3062

❸ 3mm rigid hose #75 (inside round bricks)

❹ 1x2x1 panel #4865

❺ 1x4 hinge plate #2429 with #2430

Stained Glass

Use multicolored transparent plates and slopes with tiles for a beautiful stained-glass effect. Experiment with different colors and patterns.

❶ 40 tooth gear #3649

❷ 1x1 round plate #4073

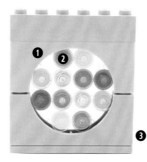

❶ 4x4 round plate #60474

❷ 1x1 round plate #4073

❸ 1x6x2 arch with thin top #12939

1x1 round plate #4073

1x1 brick #3005

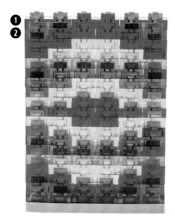

❶ 1x2 plate #3023

❷ 1x1 plate #3024

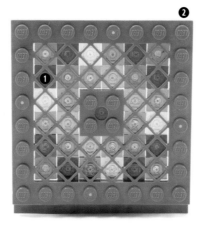

❶ 1x1 plate #3024

❷ 8x8 plate with grate #4151

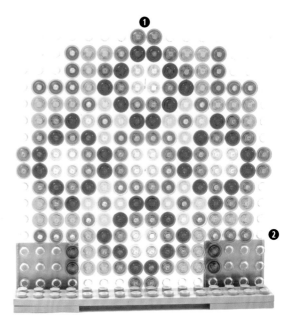

❶ 1x1 round plate #4073

❷ 16x16 baseplate #3867

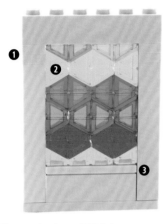

1. 1x1 plate #3024
2. 1x1 cheese slope #54200
3. 1x4 tile #2431

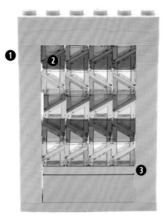

1. 1x1 plate #3024
2. 1x1 cheese slope #54200
3. 1x4 tile #2431

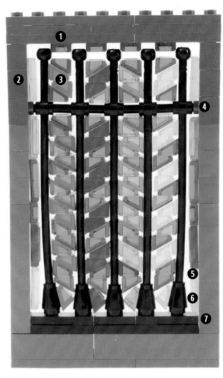

1. 1x1 tile #3070
2. 1x2 tile #3069
3. 1x1 cheese slope #54200
4. 3mm 9L rigid hose #75
5. 16L bar with towball and open stud #30219
6. 1x1 cone #4589
7. 1x2 jumper plate #3794/#15573

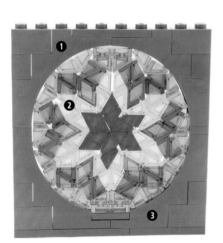

1. 1x5x4 arch #76768
2. 1x1 cheese slope #54200
3. 1x5x4 inverted arch #30099

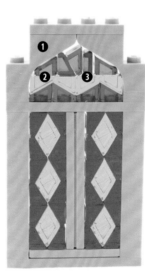

1. 1x3x2 arch #88292
2. 1x1 cheese slope #54200
3. 1x1 tile #3070

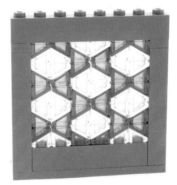

1x1 cheese slope #54200

Lattice Windows

Combine fence and fence gate pieces to re-create fancy latticework.

Mount fences using 1x1 bricks with stud on side (#87087).

Wedge the side edge between the studs of a 2x2 plate (#3022) or brick (#3003).

The 2x2 girder by Alt Bricks gives a similar effect.

How To: Ornamental Fence Latticework

You can also use 1x4x2 ornamental fences (#19121) for latticework, mounted either right-side up or upside down.

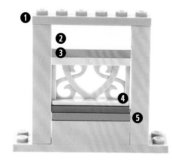

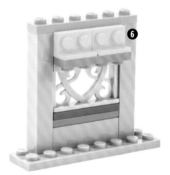

❶ 1x6 plate #3666

❷ 1x4 brick #3010

❸ 2x4 plate #3020

❹ 1x4x2 ornamental fence #19121

❺ 1x4 tile #2431

❻ 1x2 - 1x2 inverted bracket #99780

Paired fences create a central vertical line
that mimics a latticed casement window.

Use colored transparent plates or bricks behind
fence pieces to mimic stained glass.

How To: Double-Fence Latticework

The 1x1 headlight brick is key to double-fence
latticework.

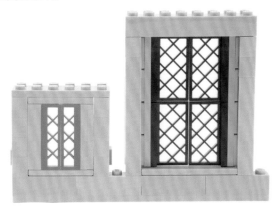

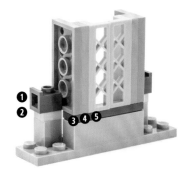

❶ 1x1 headlight brick #4070   ❹ 1x4 plate #3710

❷ 1x1 plate #3024   ❺ 1x4x1 fence #3633

❸ 2x4 plate #3020

Window Tracery

You can use a variety of pieces to add tracery to your windows, including bars with clips, plant and animal parts, minifig parts, and tools.

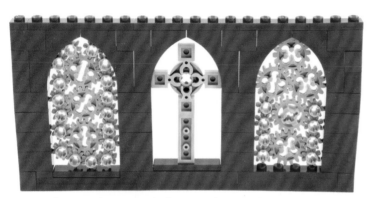

Gears, plates, and clips can be used as tracery.

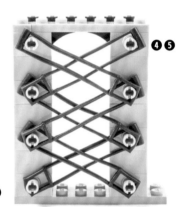

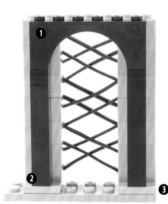

❶ 1x6x2 arch with thick top #15254

❷ 1x1x5 brick #2453

❸ 1x2 jumper plate #3794/#15573

❹ 1x2 brick with pin #2458

❺ Horse reins (by BrickForge)

❶ 1x5x4 arch #76768

❷ 1x1 tile with clip #15712

❸ 1x12x3 arch #14707

❹ 1x3x2 inverted arch #18653

❺ U-Clip (by BrickArms)

❻ Belville bib sprue #30111c01

❼ 1x3 tile #63864

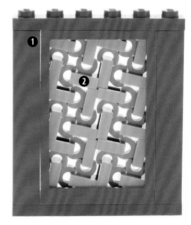

❶ 1x4x5 window #2493

❷ 1x1 tile with clip #15712

Only clips with curved sides (shown in dark red) have enough flex to clip to themselves. Clips with straight sides (shown in black) will not work with this technique.

Rose Windows

A rose window is a round window that uses radiating tracery to hold the glass.

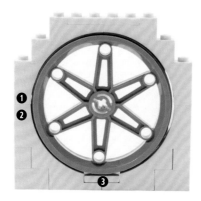

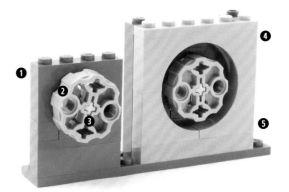

The circle created by 1x5x4 arches fits a 61.6mm wheel or an 8x8 dish.

❶ 1x5x4 arch #76768

❷ 1x5x4 inverted arch #30099

❸ 61.6mm wheel #2903

You can have the parts protrude or set back so that they are flush with the wall.

❶ 1x4x2 arch #6182

❷ Weapon barrel #98585

❸ Technic axle pin #3749

❹ 1x6x2 arch with thin top #12939

❺ 1x3x2 inverted arch #18653

❶ 1x1 round plate #4073

❷ 2x2 dish #4740

❸ 2x2 dish with cockpit printing #4740pb005

❹ Chef hat #3898

❺ 2x2 boat plate #2654

❻ 3x3 dish #43898

❼ 2x4 modified plate with curved sides #88000

❽ 4x4 dish #3960

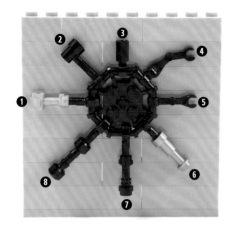

Build your own radiating tracery by attaching handles or small decorative pieces to a 2x2 plate with octagonal handles (#30033).

❶ Handle with side studs #92690

❷ 1x3 bar with clip and stud #4735

❸ Bar holder with clip #11090

❹ Robot arm bent #30377

❺ Robot arm straight #59230

❻ Telescope #64644

❼ Lightsaber hilt #64567

❽ Skateboard wheel mag #45918

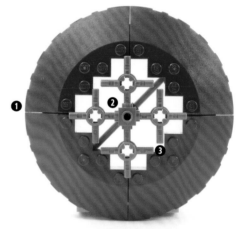

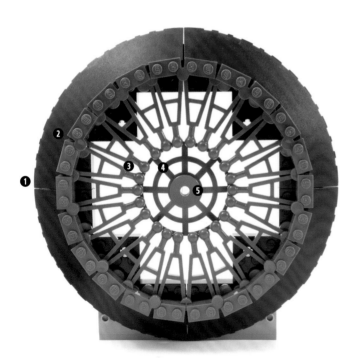

❶ 10x10 quarter dish #58846

❷ 1x4 hinge plate #2429 with #2430

❸ 1x2 modified plate with long towball #2508

❹ 6x6 dish with cutouts #4285

❺ 2x2 round tile with hole #15535

❶ 6x6 quarter dish #95188

❷ 1x1 brick with studs on 4 sides #4733

❸ Technic axle hub #48723

❹ 1x1 brick with stud on side #87087

❺ 4L bar #30374

❻ 1x1 brick with studs on 2 sides #47905

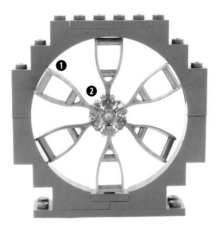

❶ Crutch #24077

❷ Weapon holder ring #20612

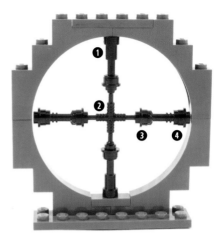

❶ Telescope #64644

❷ Wheel wrench #11402d

❸ 1x1 round plate with hollow stud #85861

❹ Lightsaber hilt #64567

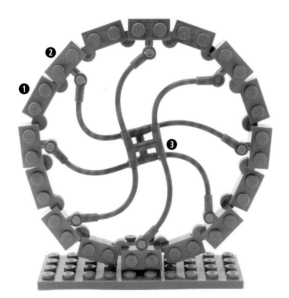

❶ 1x4 hinge plate #2429 with #2430

❷ 1x2 plate with vertical bar #4623

❸ Stretcher holder #x169

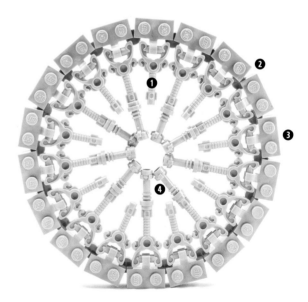

❶ Ornate key #19118

❷ 1x4 hinge plate #2429 with #2430

❸ 1x2 plate with clip #11476

❹ Lightsaber hilt #64567

Window Framing and Decor

Windowsills

A sill is the bottom ledge of a window and can be dressed up in many ways.

1x2 plate with rail #32028

1x6 double inverted slope #52501

Mechanical arm #98313

1x2 inverted slope #3665
1x3 inverted slope #4287

2x2 custom printed tile

Cat tail #15429

1x3x2 arch #88292

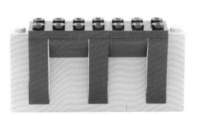

1x2x3 inverted slope #2449
2x2 inverted slope #3660

1x3x2 arch with curved top #6005

Window Trims

Trims refer to headers, jambs, and other decorations around the perimeter of a window.

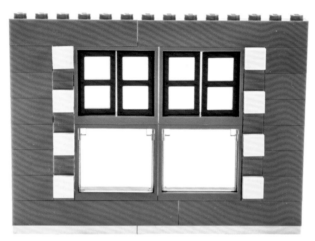

Add 1x1 tiles (#3070) in a contrasting color.

Create realistic upper and lower window sashes using setbacks at different depths.

Use plates with rail to accentuate windows that are flush with the wall.

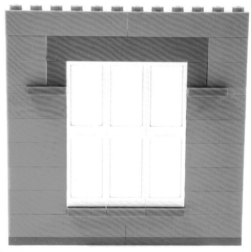

Emphasize the lintel above the window using bricks and plates in a coordinating color.

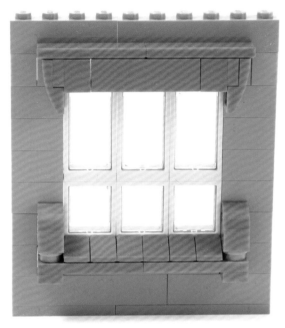

Group multiple windows within the same trim.

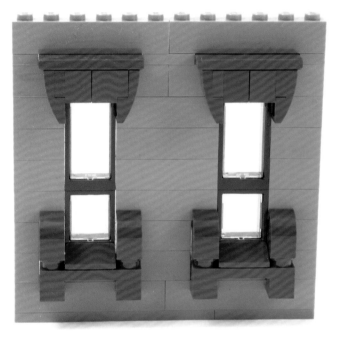

Give individual windows their own trims.

These windows are connected
by a repeating arched trim.

Recessed Panel Trims

Use panel pieces to create the look of deep-set, modern window trims.

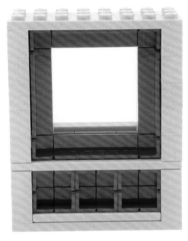

Frame an entire window with panels and extend the trim into the wall details.

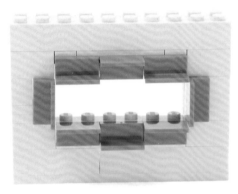

Create a pattern by placing panel pieces in alternating directions.

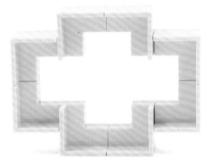

Use panel pieces to create unusually shaped trims.

Create a ledge above a window.

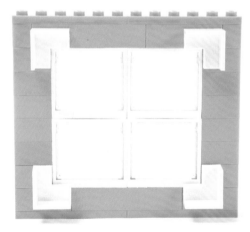

Use panel pieces to emphasize just the corners.

Combine panel pieces with wedge plates and plates with clip to create a deeply recessed window.

Side Trims

Add matching parts on each side of your windows to create support for an overhang or to emphasize the sills.

1x1 tile #3070

1x1 tile #3070

Tassel #25375

1x3 Bionicle tooth #x346

Flame #18395

Plant curved stem #28870

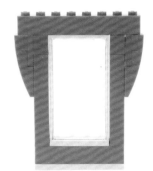

1x4 curved slope #61678

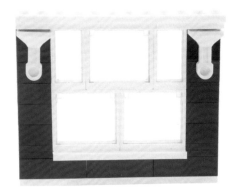

Droid leg #30362

1x3 curved slope #50950

Window Crossheads

Top your windows with crossheads—horizontal moldings that can run the length of either the window or the entire facade.

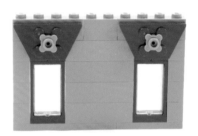

2x4 wedge plate #51739

1x1 round plate with flower edge #33291

2x2 curved slope with lip #30602

1x2 slope #3040

6x8 pointed wedge #22390

1x2x2/3 brick with wing end #47458

1x2x3 inverted slope #2449

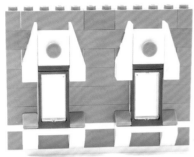

3x4 wedge #50373/#2399

Horse hitching #2397

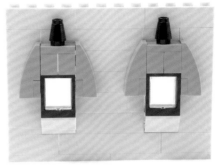

1x2 curved slope #11477

Technic gear timing wheel
8 tooth #32060

3x3 thin L-shape liftarm #32056
12-tooth gear #6589

2x3 wedge plate right/left
#43722/#43723

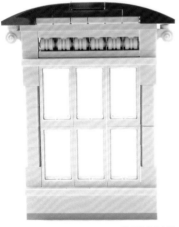

1x1 brick with scroll #20310

1x3 double inverted slope #2341

2x3x2/3 brick with wing end #47456

Arched Crossheads

Mudguards and arches make for excellent window coverings, but you can also use a variety of pieces to re-create this shape.

4 x 2 1/2 x 1 2/3 round arch
mudguard #50745

4x2 1/2x1 round arch
mudguard #98282

1 1/2x6x1 arch mudguard #62361
Small lever base #4592

1 1/2x6x1 arch mudguard #62361
1x4 curved slope #61678

1x12x3 arch #14707
1x2x1 1/3 modified brick with curved top #6091

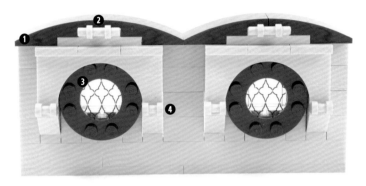

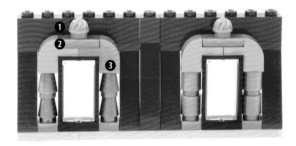

1. 1x4 curved slope #61678

2. 1x2 modified plate with handle on side #2540

3. 4x4 round plate with 2x2 hole #11833

4. 1x2 modified plate with handle on end #60478

1. 1x1 round plate with swirled top #15470

2. 1x2 jumper plate #3794/#15573

3. 1x2x1 1/3 modified brick with curved top #6091

4x4 macaroni tile #27507

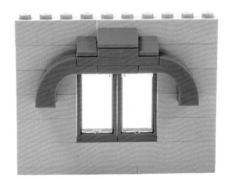

1x2 cheese slope #85984

1x1 cheese slope #54200

1x3x2 arch with curved top #6005

12L tabbed flexible hose #x131

Classical Pediments

Pediments are decorative elements that sit on top of crossheads. Classical pediments are usually made of stone and triangular in shape.

14x3x15 1/3 Scala window frame

❶ 1x2 plate with clip on top #92280

❷ 1x2 modified plate with handle on end #60478

❶ 1x2 plate with click hinge 1 finger on top #30383

❷ 1x2 plate with click hinge 2 fingers on end #44302

❸ 1x1 plate with ring #4081

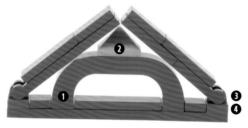

❶ 1x6x2 arch with curved top #6183

❷ 1x2 triple slope #3048/#15571

❸ 1x2 modified plate with handle on end #60478

❹ 1x1 tile with clip #2555/#15712/#93794

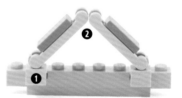

❶ 1x1 tile with clip #2555/#15712/#93794

❷ 1x2 plate with handles on 2 ends #18649

1x1 plate with ring #4081

1x2 slope #3040

1x2 inverted slope #3665

1x2 slope #3040

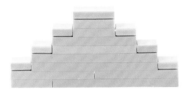

1x plates

1x tiles

Plane tail #2340

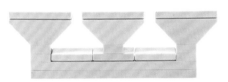

1x3 double inverted slope #2341

1x1 cheese slope #54200

1x4 curved slope #61678

1x2 double slope #3044

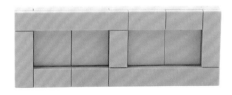

1x2 tile #3069

1x3 tile #63864

1x6 tile #6636

2x2 pentagonal wedge plate
#27928

1x1 round plate with swirled top #15470

Technic driving ring extension #32187

2x2x2 slope #3688

3x3 double convex slope #3675

Decorative Pediments

While classical pediments are usually triangular, you can use arches to create rounded variations and add interesting sculptural details for decoration as well.

Gargoyle wings (#20608) add gothic detail to your window.

1x5x4 inverted arch #30099

Ornate key #19118

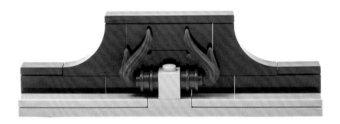

1x3x2 inverted arch #18653

Ponytail #22411

1x3x2 arch with curved top #6005

1x3x2 inverted arch #18653

Crab #33121

1x3x2 inverted arch #18653

1x1 round plate with swirled top #15470

1x1 round tile #98138

Window Pilasters

Pilasters are decorative column elements that nicely frame a window.

1x1x6 solid pillar #43888

1x1 headlight brick #4070

1x1 round plate #4073

Microfig #85863

1x1x5 1/3 spiral staircase axle #40244

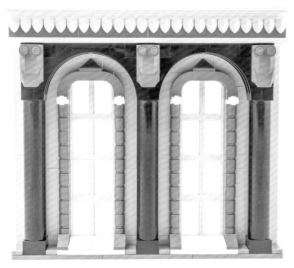

2x2x11 solid pillar #6168

1x1 round brick #3062

1x2 modified plate with socket on end #14418

Technic axle towball #2736

2L ridged axle connector #6538

Canopies and Awnings

Sloped pieces make for great canopies and awnings, which are often found over storefront windows. Awnings can add a lot of character to the exterior of a building.

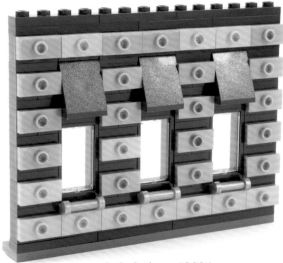

2x2x3 slope #3684

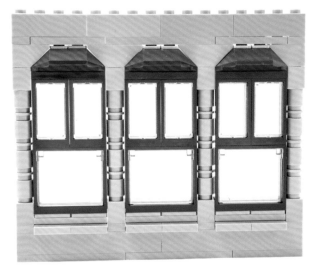

2x4 triple wedge #47759

6x2 wedge left #41748

6x2 wedge right #41747

2x2x3 1/3 octagonal brick #6037

4x2 triple wedge left/right #43710/#43711

1x2 slope #3040

2x4x2 inverted windscreen #4284

3x4x3 curved panel #18910

1x4 1/2 mudguard #50947

1x3x2 arch with curved top #6005

1x2x1 1/3 modified brick with curved top #6091

1x1 quarter round tile #25269

1x4 curved slope #61678

1x1 half rounded tile #24246

Cloth awning #45700

8L bar with stop rings and pin #2714

Doors

Basic Doors

Premade doors are the simplest way to add a door to your models. Rectangular doors fit comfortably in 1x4x6 frames, or you can use bricks to frame them.

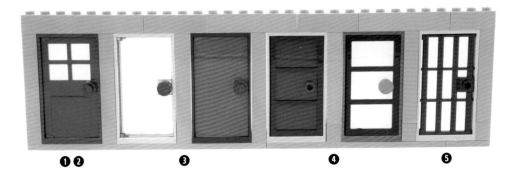

❶ 1x4x6 door with 4 panes #60623

❷ 1x4x6 door frame #30179/#60596

❸ 1x4x6 door with stud handle #60616

❹ 1x4x6 door with 3 panes #60797

❺ 1x4x6 barred door #60621

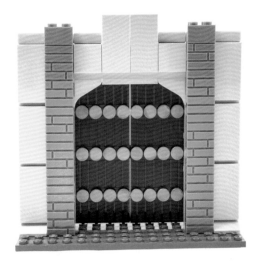
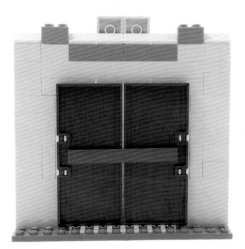

The studs on the 1x5x7 1/2 stockade door (#30223) allow for easy decoration. You can add silver 1x1 round tiles (#98138) to mimic metal studs and a 1x8 tile (#4162) across the back for a locking bar.

Arched Doors and Gates

Most arched door pieces fit onto shutter tabs, whereas gates fit onto clips.

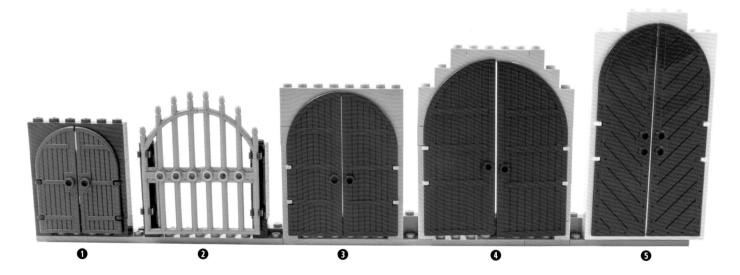

❶ 1x3x6 curved top door #2554
1x1x2 brick with shutter holder #3581
1x6x2 arch #3307/#12939/#15254

❷ 1x4x8 arched gate #42448
1x1 brick with clip #30241

❸ 1x4x8 curved top door #6105
1x1x2 brick with shutter holder #3581
1x8x2 arch #3308/#16577

❹ 1x5x10 curved top door #2400
1x1x2 brick with shutter holder #3581
1x5x4 arch #2339/#76768

❺ 1x4x11 1/3 arched top door #33216
1x10x12 door frame #33240

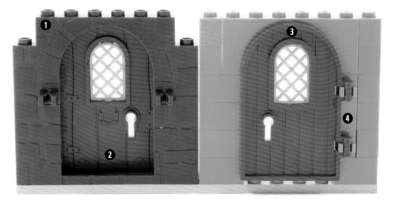

The 1x4x6 round top door has two variants:
one has shutter tabs that can be attached directly
to a door frame, while the other has handles
to clip onto bricks with clips.

❶ 1x8x6 door frame #40242

❷ 1x4x6 round top door #40241

❸ 1x4x6 round top door with reinforced edge #64390

❹ 1x1x3 brick with 2 clips #60583

Dutch Doors

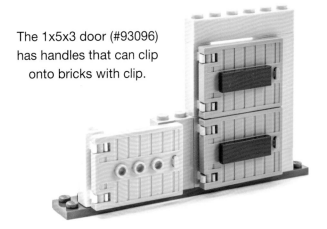

The 1x5x3 door (#93096) has handles that can clip onto bricks with clip.

These left-handed and right-handed doors have studs that act as hinges.

❶ 1x3x2 door left/right #3189/#3188

❷ 1x3x1 door left/right #3822/#3821

Sliding and Revolving Doors

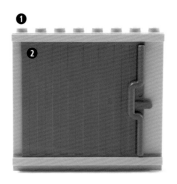

Use 2x8 plates with wide rail to make a door slide. Some sliding doors are thin enough to fit on a 1x8 plate with rail (#4510).

❶ 2x8 plate with wide rail #30586

❷ Sliding door #4511

❸ 1x4x6 door with 4 panes #60623

Four doors can be arranged on an 8x8 round tile (#6177) to look like a revolving door.

Custom Doors

Depending on the scale of your model, you can also build your own doors. Stagger tiles to make wooden doors, or create custom paneled, round, or even sliding doors.

❶ 1x2x3 panel with side supports #87544

❷ 1x1 round plate with swirled top #15470

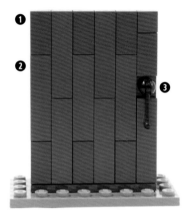

❶ 1x2 tile #3069

❷ 1x4 tile #2431

❸ Small lever #4592 with #4593

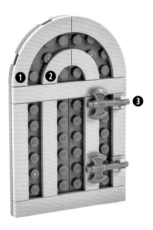

❶ 4x4 macaroni tile #27507

❷ 2x2 macaroni tile #27925

❸ Twin-blade axe #94158f

Repurpose unexpected pieces to create door hinges and handles.

❶ Binoculars #30162

❷ Skateboard wheel mag #45918

Custom Hinges

Build your own hinges to add character to your doors.

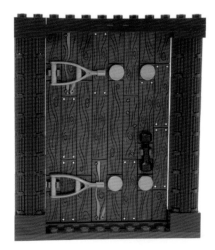

Plate pieces with handles, clips, and other connectors can be used to create functional hinges for attaching a custom-built door.

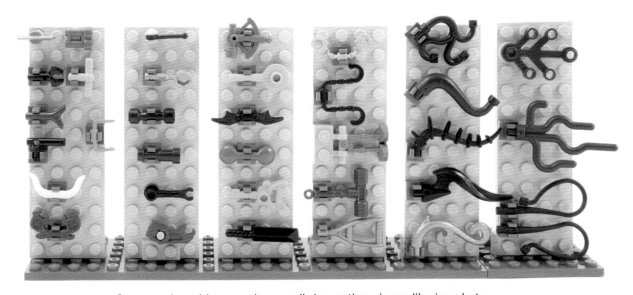

Create unique hinges using small decorative pieces like ice skates (#93555), bucket handles (#95344), carrot tops (#33183), mechanical arms (#53989/#98313), signal paddles (#3900), and more.

Garage Doors

Rolltop and carriage-style garage doors can be made from window frames or plate panels.

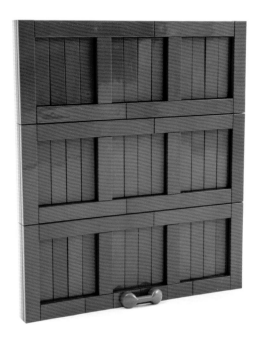

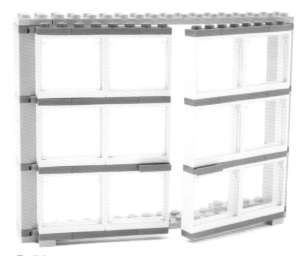

Build a carriage-style garage door using plates with hinge and 1x4x3 windows (#60594).

Build a rolltop-style garage door with or without windows.

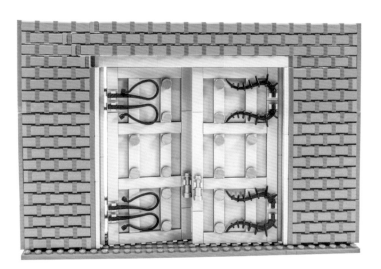

Decorate carriage doors with oversize hinges.

Entryways

Here are some ways to incorporate your doors into your builds.

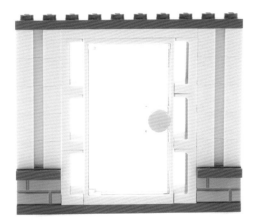

Integrate doors with sidelight windows.

Integrate the doorway into retaining walls.

Windows on each side add symmetry
to this entryway.

Frame a doorway with a pediment and
columns for a neoclassical look.

Grand Gates

Here are some ideas and parts to create a dramatic entryway.

1x3x6 curved top door #2554

1x8x3 curved fence bar #95229

A grand entrance fit for a castle.

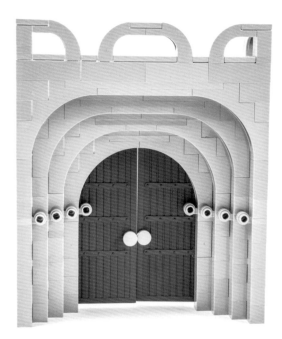

Layer surrounding walls for emphasis.

Portcullises

Use bricks with groove to guide a portcullis that you can raise and lower.

❶ 1x2x5 modified brick with groove #88393

❷ 1x8x12 portcullis #89519

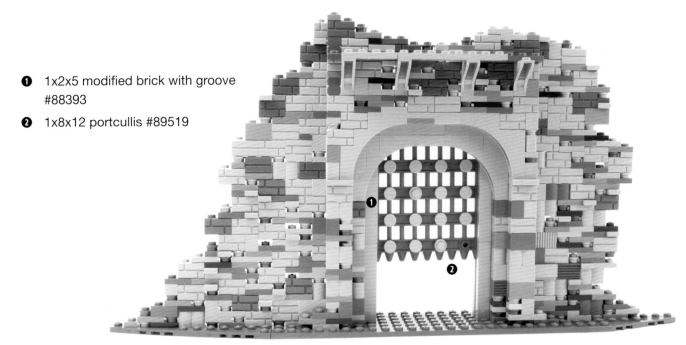

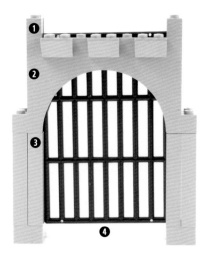

❶ 1x2 modified brick with groove #4216

❷ 2x12x6 arch #30272

❸ 1x2x5 modified brick with groove #88393

❹ 9x13 bar grill #6046

Build your own portcullis to fit an opening of any size or scale.

❶ Weapon pike with 4 side blades #43899

❷ Hero Factory ammo belt #98567

Column Bases

The base of a column is usually broader than the shaft it supports. It can be fluted, square, or round.

❶ 2x2x11 solid pillar #6168

❷ 1x1 round plate with flower edge #33291

❸ 1x5x4 inverted arch #30099

❶ 1x1x6 solid pillar #43888

❷ 1x1x5 brick #2453

❸ 1x3 curved slope #50950

❹ 1x4 curved slope #61678

❶ 1x2 cheese slope #85984

❷ 2x2 double concave slope #3046

❸ 1x2 slope #3040

❹ 1x1 cheese slope #54200

2x2 pentagonal wedge plate #27928

❶ 6x6 tile with 4 studs #45522

❷ 1x2x3 slope #4460

❶ 4x4x2 cone #3943

❷ 4x4 round brick #87081

❸ Bionicle canister lid #47491

❹ 3x3x2 cone #6233

❺ 5x5 dish #6942

Round Shafts

The shaft is the part of the column between the base and the capital.

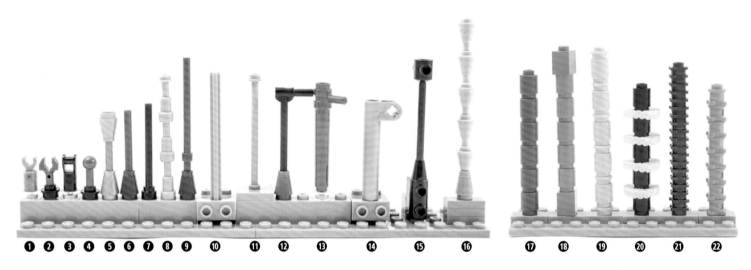

1. Bar holder with clip #11090

2. 1L bar with clip mechanical claw #48729

3. Bar holder with handle #23443

4. 1L bar with towball #22484

5. 1x1 cone #4589
   4L bar #30374

6. 1x1 cone #4589
   4L bar #30374

7. 1x4 antenna #3957

8. Telescope #64644

9. 1x1 cone #4589
   6L bar with stop ring #63965

10. 5L axle #32073

11. 2x2 tile with bar and stud #98549

12. 5L bar with handle #87618

13. 1x5 1/2 cylinder with handle #87617

14. Axle and pin connector with extension #53586

15. 1x8 bar with 1x2 brick #30359

16. Ice cream cone #11610

17. 1x1 round brick #3062

18. 1x1 brick #3005
    1x1 round brick #3062

19. 1x1 round brick #3062
    1x1 round plate #4073

20. 1x1 round brick #3062
    Ruff #99251

21. 1x1 round plate with flower edge #33291

22. 1x1 round brick with flower edge #33286

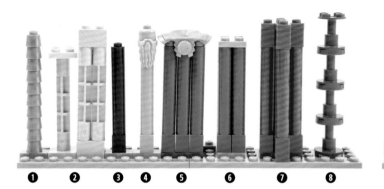

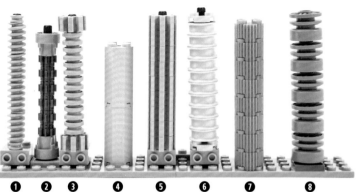

❶ Fez #85975

❷ 1x1x5 1/3 spiral staircase axle #40244

❸ 1x1x6 solid pillar #43888

❹ 1x1x6 solid pillar #43888
Beard #10052
Head #3626

❺ 1x1x6 solid pillar #43888
Minifig armor shoulder pads #15066

❻ 1x1x6 solid pillar #43888
2x2 plate #3022

❼ 1x1x6 solid pillar #43888
3x3 plate cross #15397

❽ 2x2x2 support with stand #3940

❶ Technic gear worm screw long #4716

❷ Technic gear 8 tooth type 2 #10928
Technic driving ring extension #32187

❸ Technic gear timing wheel 8 tooth #32060
11mm x 8mm wheel with groove #42610

❹ 2x2x3 1/3 octagonal brick #6037

❺ Technic gear timing wheel 8 tooth #32060

❻ 2x2 wheel spoked with pin hole #30155

❼ 2x2 round brick with flutes #92947

❽ 18mm x 14mm wheel with pin hole #55981

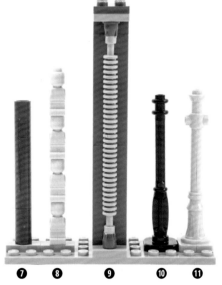

❶ Technic 1/2 bush #4265

❷ Technic bush #3713

❸ 2L axle connector #6538

❹ 2L ridged axle connector #6538

❺ Driving ring connector #18948

❻ 1L pin connector #18654

❼ 2L pin connector #75535

❽ Microfig #85863

❾ 12L tabbed flexible hose #x131

❿ 2x2x7 lamppost #2039

⓫ BrickForge lamppost

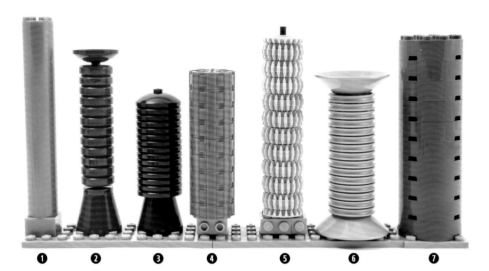

❶ 2x2 round plate #4032

❷ 2x2 round brick #3941

❸ 2x2 plate #3022
2x2 round brick #3941

❹ 2x2 dish #4740

❶ 2x2x11 solid pillar #6168

❷ 3x3 dish #43898
Wheel hockey puck #47576
2x2 round tile with stud #18674
3x3x2 cone #6233

❸ 3x3 dish #43898
3x3x2 cone #6233

❹ Weapon barrel #98585

❺ Bevel gear #32198
Double bevel gear #32269

❻ 5x5 dish #6942
Pulley #4185

❼ 4x4 round brick #87081

Balusters

Balusters are small decorative columns used to support railings or parapets.

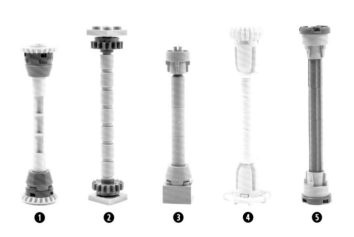

❶ 1x1x5 1/3 spiral staircase axle #40244
Bevel gear #32198
2x2 truncated cone #98100

❷ 1x1 round brick #3062
Gear with clutch #6542

❸ 2L Technic pin connector #62462
Technic driving ring extension #32187

❹ 1x1 round brick #3062
Double bevel gear #32269
2x2x2 dome with cross cut slots #33287
2x2 dish #4740

❺ 2L axle connector #6538
2x2 round tile with stud #18674

Multiple Shafts

Make wider columns from multiple shafts or from parts that have built-in symmetry.

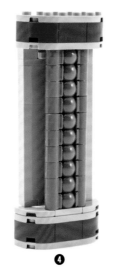

❶ 1x1 brick with scroll #20310
1x1x6 solid pillar #43888

❷ 1x1 round brick #3062
1x2 plate #3023

❸ 1x5 1/2 cylinder with handle #87617
1x2 liftarm #43857

❹ 1x3 liftarm with ball joint #98577

❶

❷

❸

❹

❶ 2L axle connector #6538

❷ 2L axle connector #6538
#1 angled axle connector #32013

❸ 1x1 round brick #3062
4x4 round plate #60474

❹ Bar holder with clip #11090
6L bar with stop ring #63965
1x2 thin liftarm #41677

❶

❷

❸

❹

Square Shafts

Add interest to square shafts by incorporating round pieces, pieces with handles or clips, and grooved pieces to mimic the look of classical fluting.

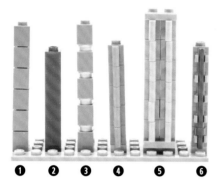

❶ 1x1 brick #3005, with small gaps between each brick

❷ 1x1x5 brick #2453

❸ 1x1 brick #3005
1x1 round plate #4073

❹ 1x1 brick with handle #2921

❺ 1x1 brick with handle #2921
1x2 plate with rail #32028

❻ 1x1 brick with clip #30241
6L bar with stop ring #63965

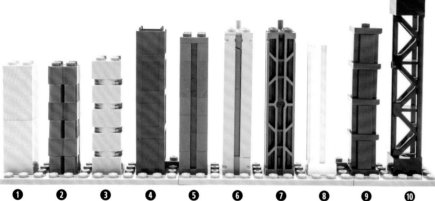

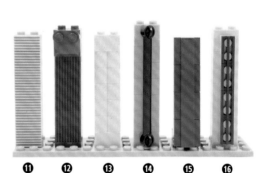

❶ 2x2x3 brick #30145

❷ 1x2 modified log brick #30136

❸ 2x2 brick #3003
2x2 round plate #4032

❹ 2x2x2 container #61780

❺ 1x2 modified brick with groove #4216

❻ 2x2x8 support with grooves #30646b

❼ 2x2x8 support with grooves and lattice on 2 sides #30646a

❽ 2x2x8 Scala support with grooves #x7

❾ 1x1 brick with studs on 4 sides #4733
1x2 tile #3069
2x2 jumper plate #87580

❿ 2x2x10 support girder type 4 #95347

⓫ 1x2 modified brick with grill #2877

⓬ 1x2 modified brick with grill #2877
2x2 modified brick with sloped end #47457

⓭ 1x2 modified log brick #30136
1x2 brick #3004

⓮ 1x2 Technic brick #3700
Technic pin with towball #6628
1x9 Technic link #32293

⓯ 2x2 jumper plate #87580
1x8 tile #4162
1x2 brick with 2 studs on side #11211

⓰ 1x2 Technic brick #3700
Half pin #4274
1x8 plate #3460
1x2 grill plate #2412

❶

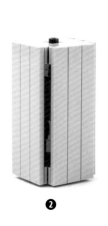

❷

❸

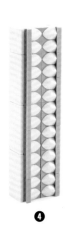

❹

❺

❻

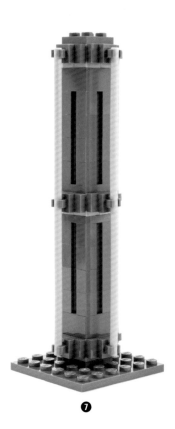

❼

❶ 1x2 cheese slope #85984

❷ 1x1 brick with studs on 4 sides #4733
1x3 double inverted slope #2341
1x8 tile #4162

❸ 1x2 jumper plate #3794/#15573
1x6 tile #6636
1x1 brick with stud on 2 adjacent sides #26604

❹ 1x1 modified plate with vertical tooth #15070
1x2 plate with rail #32028
2x4 tile #87079
2x2 tile #3068

❺ 2x2 Technic brick with ball receptacle #92013

❻ 2x3 plate #3021
1x2 jumper plate #3794/#15573
1x2 modified brick with grill #2877
1x2 tile with groove #3069

❼ 2x2 modified brick with grooves and axle hole #90258
1x2 jumper plate #3794/#15573
1x1 brick with stud on 2 adjacent sides #26604
1x1 tile with clip #15712
16L 3mm rigid hose #75
6x6 plate #3958

Decorative Shafts

Use decorative elements to add unexpected flourishes to the shafts of your columns, or use tiles to build faceted shafts for a more modern look.

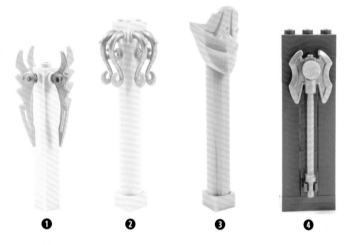

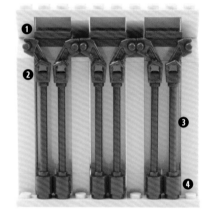

❶ Weapon crescent blade #98141

❷ Plant curved stem #28870

❸ Hero Factory Shoulder Armor #15369

❹ Twin bladed axe head #11096

❶ 1x2 modified plate with handles #3839

❷ Mechanical arm #53989/#98313

❸ 6.6L bar with stop ring #4095

❹ 1x1 round brick #3062

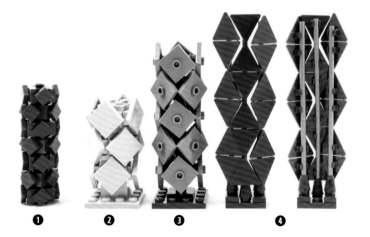

Faceted shafts work well without bases or capitals.

❶ 1x1 brick with studs on 4 sides #4733
1x2 jumper plate #3794/#15573
1x1 tile #3070

❷ 2x2 tile #3068

❸ 2x2 jumper plate #87580

❹ 2x2 triangular sign #892

Capitals

A column's capital sits on top of the shaft and is typically broader than the shaft to support the entablature above.

Short droid leg #17486

The base can be mirrored in the capital, like with this propeller housing (#6040).

Minifigure legs #970c00

2x2 square flag #2335

Lightsaber hilt #64566

Mechanical arm #53989/#98313

Doric Capitals

Create simple Doric capitals with slope and wedge pieces.

1x2 curved slope #11477

2x2 curved slope #15068

1x3 double inverted slope #2341

2x4 triple wedge #47759

1x1 cheese slope #54200

1x2 curved slope #11477

2x2 inverted slope,
double convex #3676

2x2 inverted slope,
double convex #3676

Ionic Capitals

Re-create the look of Ionic capitals with 1x1 bricks with scroll (#20310).

- ❶ 1x1 brick with scroll #20310
- ❷ 4x4 plate #3031

- ❶ 1x1 brick with scroll #20310
- ❷ 1x2 jumper plate #3794/#15573

- ❶ 1x1 brick with scroll #20310
- ❷ Cat tail #15429

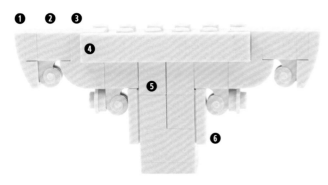

- ❶ 1x2 curved slope #11477
- ❷ 1x1 brick with scroll #20310
- ❸ 1x2x1 1/3 modified brick with curved top #6091
- ❹ 1x6 tile #6636
- ❺ 1x1 brick with stud on side #87087
- ❻ 1x2 tile #3069

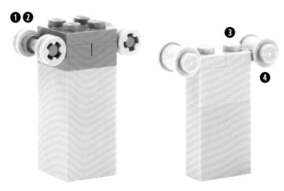

You can also use Technic pieces and plates with ring to mimic this effect.

- ❶ 1x2 modified plate with handle on side #2540
- ❷ Technic 1/2 bush #4265
- ❸ 1x1 round plate #4073
- ❹ 1x1 plate with ring #4081

Corinthian Capitals

You can use curved slopes and arches to emphasize the four corners of a capital, hinting at a Corinthian design.

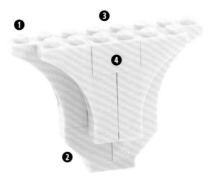

❶ 1x3x3 arch #13965

❷ 1x2 inverted slope #3665

❸ 1x4 brick #3010

❹ 1x2 brick #3004

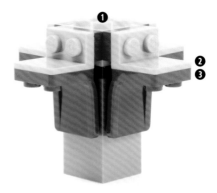

❶ 1x1 brick with stud on 2 adjacent sides #26604

❷ 1x2 - 2x2 inverted bracket #99207

❸ 2x2 minifig utensil seat #4079

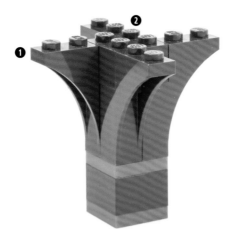

❶ 1x3x3 arch #13965

❷ 2x2 brick #3003

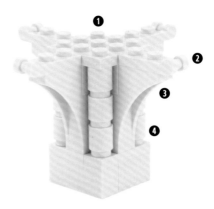

❶ 3x3 plate #11212

❷ 1x2 modified plate with handle on end #60478

❸ 1x3x3 arch #13965

❹ 1x1 round brick with open stud #3062

Decorative Capitals

Custom decorative capitals can be colorful and playful.

❶

❷

❸

❹

❺

❻

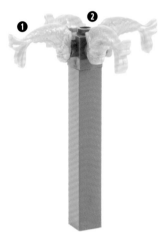

❶ Ornamental fish #x59

❷ 1x1 brick with studs on 4 sides #4733

❸ 1x2x5 modified brick with groove #88393

❶ Crab #33121

❷ 2x3x3 modified brick with cutout and lion head #30274

❸ Antler #11437

❹ 2x3x2/3 brick with wing end #47456
1x1 round tile #98138
Plant vine #55236
2x2 inverted slope #3660

❺ Pentagonal shield #22408
1x1 modified plate with horizontal tooth #49668

❻ Bionicle chest cover #49423

❶

❷

❸

❹

Even a small column can have a custom capital!

❶ 1x2 modified plate with socket on end #14418
1x2 modified plate with socket on side #14704

❷ 2x2 round brick with petal base #15469

❸ Crown with 4 spikes #18165

❹ Zabrak horns #95747

Connected Columns

Connect your columns using arch and tile pieces as entablatures to build a grand archway or a colonnade.

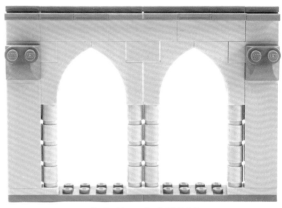

1x3x3 arch #13965

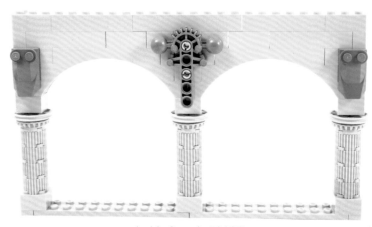

1x12x3 arch #6108

1x5x4 arch #2339

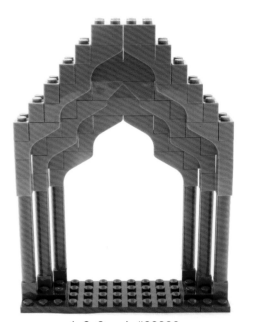

1x3x2 arch #88292

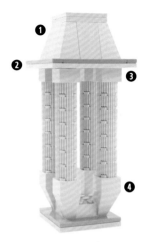

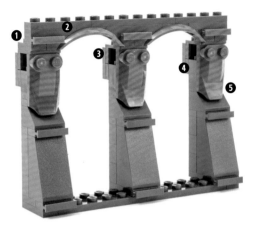

1. 2x3x3 modified brick with cutout and lion head #30274
2. 1x2 modified plate with socket on end #14418
3. Technic axle towball #2736

1. 2x2x3 double convex slope #3685
2. 6x6 plate #3958
3. 2x2 brick #3003
4. 6x6x2 inverted slope with cutouts #30373

1. 1x2 plate with rail #32028
2. 1 1/2x6x1 arch mudguard #62361
3. 1x2 - 2x2 bracket #44728
4. 1x2x1 2/3 brick with studs on 1 side #22885
5. 2x3x2/3 brick with wing end #47456

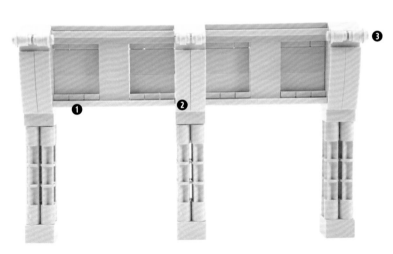

1. 1x2 jumper plate #3794/#15573
2. 1x4 curved slope #61678
3. 1x1 plate with ring #4081

1. Hero Factory handcuff #98562
2. 1x6x3 1/3 arch with curved top #6060

Towers

Stacked Towers

Stack bricks or plates in alternating layers to create a subtly textured tower. The larger the diameter of your circle, the smoother the exterior becomes.

2x2 corner plate #2420

2x2 round plate #4032

When using 2x2 bricks (#3003), fill in the space of the protruding stud with 1x1 round bricks (#3062).

Building a tower with 2x3 wedge bricks (#6565/#6564) can be delicate in the beginning as the pieces aren't fully connected to one another. But as you build higher, the tower becomes more stable.

Liftarm Towers

Connect liftarms with pins to form any tower-like shape.

Create a simple octagonal tower by alternating 1x3 liftarms (#32523) and 1x5 liftarms (#32316).

Layer 3x3 T-shape liftarms (#60484) with staggered pins to form a tower with protruding corners.

How To

The longer the liftarms, the larger your tower will be. Add or remove sides to change the shape.

❶ 1x3 liftarm #32523

❷ 1x5 liftarm #32316

❸ 3L pin #6558

❹ 3L pin without ridges #32556

Brick with Stud Towers

Use bricks with studs on side as a central column and then attach exterior plates or tiles.

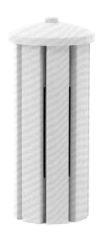

❶ 1x2 plate #3023

❷ 1x4 plate #3710

❸ 1x1 round plate #4073

❹ 1x1 brick with studs on 4 sides #4733

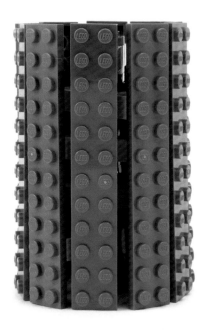

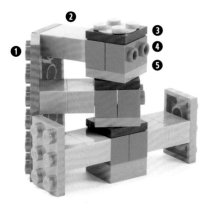

❶ 2x plates

❷ 1x2 brick #3004

❸ Turntable #3679 with #3680

❹ 1x2 brick with 2 studs on side #11211

❺ 2x2 plate #3022

Curved Slope Towers

Arrange curved slopes around a core of plates with handle and plates with clips to create towers with smooth, rounded exteriors.

2x2 curved slope #15068

2x4 curved slope #88930

How To

You can use any length of 2x bricks and plates and build this tower as high as you want.

❶ 2x2 curved slope #15068

❷ 2x brick

❸ 1x2 plate with handle on side #48336

❹ 1x2 plate with 2 clips #60470

❺ 2x plate

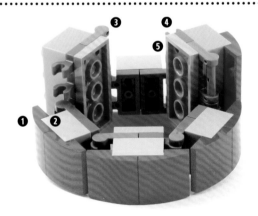

Small Curved Slope Towers

Bracket pieces are the key to making a compact tower of these 2x2 curved slopes.

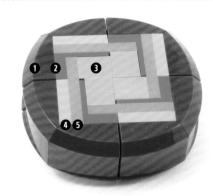

❶ 2x2 curved slope with lip #30602

❷ 1x2 - 2x2 bracket #44728

❸ 1x2 brick #3004

❹ 2x2 plate #3022

❺ 2x3 plate #3021

Large Curved Slope Towers

Connect long curved slopes with the 1x1 brick with studs on 4 sides for a tower with a larger diameter.

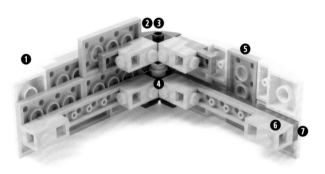

❶ 2x4 curved slope #93606

❷ 1x2 cheese slope #85984

❸ 1x1 brick with studs on 4 sides #4733

❹ 1x1 round plate #4073

❺ 2x4 plate #3020

❻ 1x1 headlight brick #4070

❼ 1x8 plate #3460

Tower Bases

Combine regular plates with A-shape, wedge, or hinge plates to create the circular base for a tower.

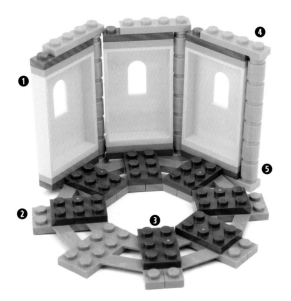

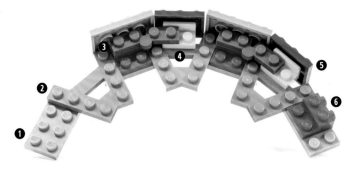

❶ 1x4x5 panel with window #60808

❷ A-shape plate #15706

❸ 2x3 plate #3021

❹ 1x4 plate #3710

❺ 1x1 round brick #3062

❶ 2x4 plate #3020

❷ A-shape plate #15706

❸ 1x4 hinge plate #2429 with #2430

❹ 1x2 - 1x2 inverted bracket #99780

❺ 2x3 plate #3021

❻ 2x2x2/3 modified plate #99206

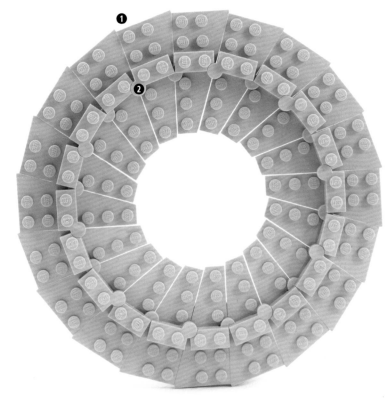

When creating a tower base with wedge plates, the hinge plates that connect them can be placed on top of or below the wedge plates.

❶ 6x3 wedge plate left #54384

❷ 1x4 hinge plate #2429 with #2430

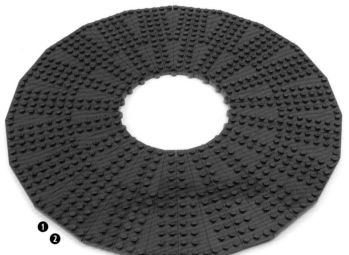

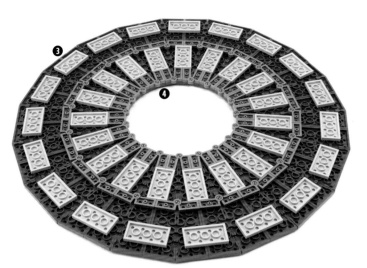

❶ 3x12 wedge plate left #47397

❷ 3x12 wedge plate right #47398

❸ 2x4 plate #3020

❹ 1x4 hinge plate #2429 with #2430

Hinge Towers

Hinge plates and hinge bricks give you lots of flexibility in a tower. You can even add decorative quoins to emphasize each corner.

Add visual interest with textured bricks like the 1x2 modified log brick (#30136).

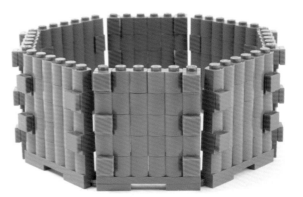

Use 1x1 bricks with stud on side (#87087) with 1x1 tiles (#3070) to re-create decorative quoins.

How To: Hinge Brick Quoins

Hinge bricks can perform double duty as connectors and decorative quoins.

❶ 1x4 hinge brick #3830 with #3831

❷ 1x bricks

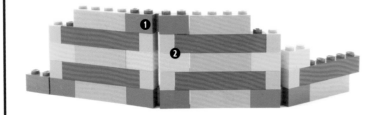

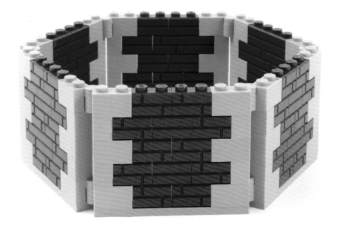

Towers with Reinforced Quoins

The base of each corner of this tower is a triangle made up of three hinge plates. Bricks with studs form the walls, which are finished with tiles.

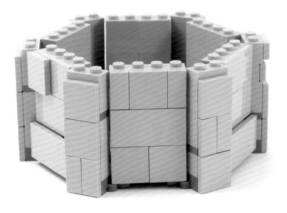

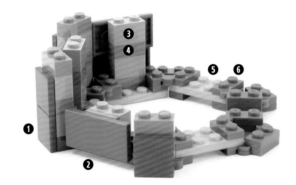

- **❶** 2x2 tile #3068
- **❷** 2x4 tile #87079
- **❸** 1x2 brick with 2 studs on side #11211
- **❹** 1x2 plate #3023
- **❺** 2x4 plate #3020
- **❻** 1x4 hinge plate #2429 with #2430

Finger Hinge Towers

Hinge bricks with fingers click into place, creating a fixed angle. The 2x6 plates hold the rows together, and the 1x2 bricks provide support between the layers of hinge bricks.

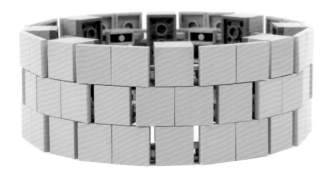

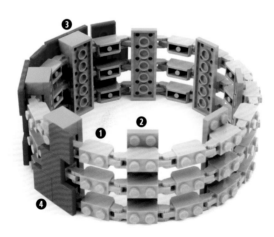

- **❶** 1x2 hinge brick locking with fingers #30386
- **❷** 2x6 plate #3795
- **❸** 1x2 brick #3004
- **❹** 2x2 tile #3068

Hinge and Bracket Towers

This massive tower uses hinge bricks to create its curved walls, and then the exterior is covered with tiles.

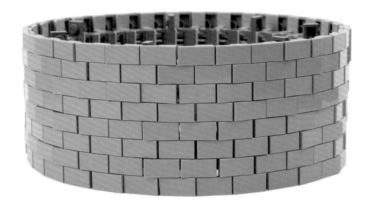

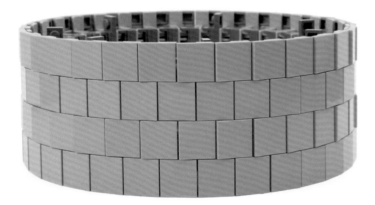

Attach brackets to the hinge bricks and then finish with 1x2 or 2x2 tiles.

❶ 1x2 tile #3069

❷ 2x2 tile #3068

❸ 1x2 - 1x4 bracket #2436

❹ 2x2 hinge brick top #6134

❺ 1x2 hinge brick base #3937

Cheese Slope Towers

Use plates with clips and handles to create the angle needed to match up cheese slopes at each corner of these towers.

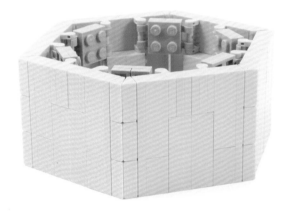

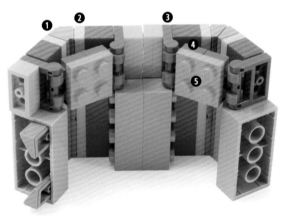

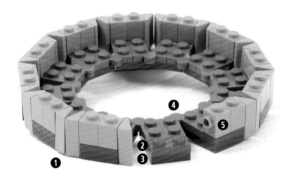

Using a single color scheme creates a smooth finish that looks like masonry.

❶ 1x2 cheese slope #85984

❷ 1x6 plate #3666

❸ 1x2 plate with handle on side #48336

❹ 1x2 plate with 2 clips #60470

❺ 2x2 plate #3022

Compared to the 6-sided version, this tower features subtler corner angles.

❶ 1x2 cheese slope #85984

❷ 1x2 plate #3023

❸ 2x3 plate #3021

❹ 1x4 hinge plate #2429 with #2430

❺ 1x1 brick with stud on side #87087

Cheese Slope and Vertical Plate Towers

This tower is built sideways by layering cheese slopes, regular plates, plates with clips, and plates with handles.

Stagger plates of varying lengths to keep the tower stable, and mix in 1x1 round plates (#4073) for a more weathered look.

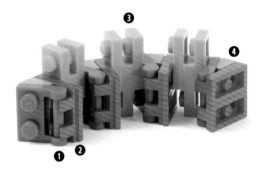

❶ 1x2 plate with handle on side #48336
❷ 1x2 plate with clip on top #92280
❸ 1x2 plate #3023
❹ 1x2 cheese slope #85984

Cheese Slope and Hinge Brick Towers

Combine cheese slopes with hinge bricks to create a round base for this tower and then cover the hinge brick tops with tiles.

❶ 1x2 hinge brick base #3937
❷ 2x2 hinge brick top #6134
❸ 1x2 plate #3023
❹ 1x2 cheese slope #85984
❺ 1x2 - 2x2 inverted bracket #99207
❻ 2x4 tile #87079

Bracket Towers

Use brackets to create the structure of a tower and then cover the sides with plates, tiles, or slopes.

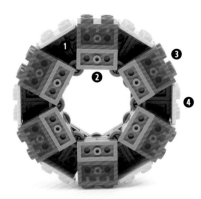

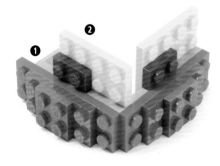

Arrange hinge plates into hexagons and then alternate layers of brackets and inverted brackets to make a 12-sided tower.

❶ 1x4 hinge plate #2429 with #2430

❷ 1x2 plate #3023

❸ 1x2 - 2x2 inverted bracket #99207

❹ 1x2 - 2x2 bracket #44728

Brackets connect four sides built by layering plates, creating a tower that can then be covered with tiles or shingles.

❶ 1x2 - 2x2 bracket #44728

❷ 2x plates

Axle Towers

Attach axles to a central, vertical axle to create the skeleton of a tower, and then cover the exterior with plates or tiles.

You can adjust the diameter of the tower by changing the length of the radiating axles. The smallest tower you can create with this method uses the triple axle hub (#57585).

Bushes hold the triple axle-pin connectors in place. Each exterior plate needs two points of connection to the central axle.

❶ 2x6 plate #3795
❷ 1x1 cone #4589
❸ Triple axle-pin connector #10288
❹ Technic 1/2 bush #4265

How To: Hose Towers

Using the Technic axle hub makes a tower with eight sides.

❶ 2x6 plate #3795
❷ 1x1 round plate #4073
❸ 1x1 cone #4589
❹ Technic axle hub #48723
❺ 3mm rigid hose #75

Clip-on Plate Towers

This tower uses a hose at the center, with clip-on plates and brackets that fan outward. Use tiles to finish the exterior.

How To

Attach 1x2 plates with clip to the center hose and then back them with 1x4 plates. Then attach 2x3 plates to the top and bottom to create radiating leaves. Then add 1x2 - 2x2 brackets.

❶ 3mm rigid hose #75

❷ 1x2 plate with clip horizontal on end #63868

❸ 1x4 plate #3710

❹ 2x3 plate #3021

❺ 1x2 - 2x2 bracket #44728

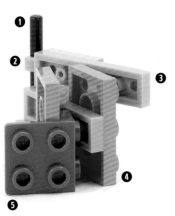

Basic Roofs

Sloped Roofs

One of the simplest ways to create a roof is to stack slopes directly on top of your walls.

1x2x2/3 slope with cutout #92946

1x2x2/3 slope with 4 slots #61409

1x2 inverted double slope #3049

Create a graphic design with printed slopes like these green-and-yellow 2x3 slopes (#3298).

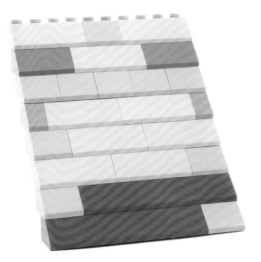

Mix slopes of different sizes to get staggered seams.

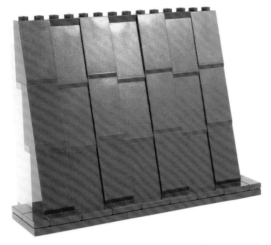

Offset slopes by a plate for subtle variation in pattern.

Alternate slopes of different sizes and colors.

Combine slopes of different angles
to create a curving roofline.

Alternate slopes and inverted slopes on
their backs for a roof with a shallower pitch.

You don't need to build with slopes
to the very top.

Create a mansard roof by combining 2x2x3 slopes (#3684)
and 2x2x3 double convex slopes (#3685).

2x2 corner slope #13548

5x6 hexagonal flag #x1435

2x2x3 double convex slope #3685

2x2x3 double convex slope #3685

2x2x2 slope #3688

Use a large slope, like this 6x8 slope (#4515), to create a simple shed roof.

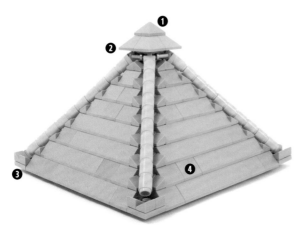

Emphasize the corners of this pyramid roof using round bricks.

❶ 1x2 triple slope #3048

❷ 2x2 double convex slope #3045

❸ 1x1 cheese slope #54200

❹ 2x2 slope #3039

Small windows add interest and color to a sloped hip roof.

Add some curves and texture to your roof with the 1x4 inverted curved slope (#13547).

Create a stepped hip roof with 1x2x2/3 bricks with wing end (#47458).

Stagger 1x2x2/3 bricks with wing end (#47458) to create a textured roof.

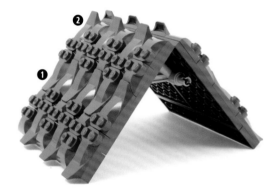

❶ 2x3x2/3 brick with wing end #47456

❷ 2x2x2/3 modified brick with sloped end #47457

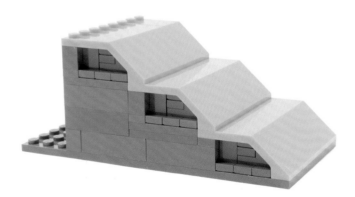

Use 2x5x1 2/3 windscreens (#6070) to create a continuous slope with no visible studs.

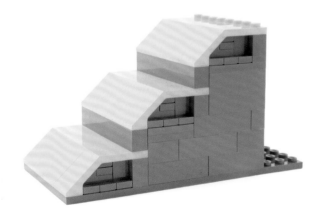

Add a layer of bricks between windscreens to create a contrasting trim.

Roof Corners

Combine slopes in different ways to negotiate the interior and exterior corners.

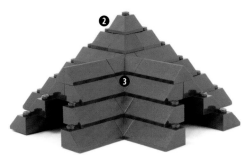

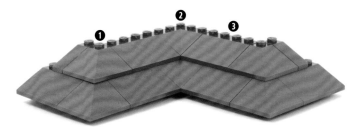

❶ 3x3 double convex slope #3675

❷ 3x3 double concave slope #99301

❸ 3x4 slope #3297

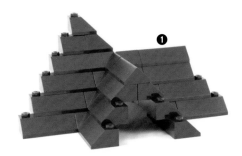

❶ 2x4 double slope #3041

❷ 2x2 double convex slope #3045

❸ 2x2 double concave slope #3046

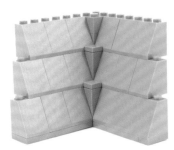

2x2x2 slope #3678

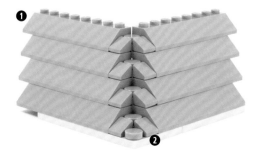

❶ 2x8 slope #4445

❷ 1x1 cheese slope #54200

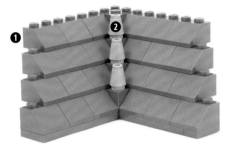

❶ 2x2 slope #3039

❷ 1x1 cone #4589

Roof Supports

Although sloped roofs are fairly stable on their own, you can reinforce them with brackets and other pieces.

Stepped brackets make a good base for a roof.

❶ 3x2x1 1/3 bracket #18671

❷ 5x2x1 1/3 bracket #11215

❸ 5x2x2 1/3 bracket #6087

You can also use 7x4x6 straight stairs (#30134) to support 45-degree slopes.

Combine bricks and plates with handle to form a triangular roof support.

Stepped Roofs

Stacking staggered layers of bricks, plates, or tiles can create an interesting pyramid-like hip roof or a simpler gable-style roof.

Staggering bricks creates a simple stepped roof design or the base for a more intricate roof design.

Use 1x1 round plates (#4073) to make a textured hip roof.

Stack jumper plates and tiles to create a smooth gabled roof.

Or stagger 1x2 and 2x2 jumper plates and then finish with tiles for a sleek look.

Mix plates and tiles, and to add interest, leave some pieces not firmly pressed down.

2x8 plate with wide rail #30586

Alternate between regular plates and plates with rail for a steeper roofline.

Shingle Roofs

Tiles make for great shingles, but you can also use plates, slopes, plants, and other unusual parts for even more variation.

Stagger tiles of different lengths, like 1x2 tiles (#3069), 1x3 tiles (#63864), and 1x4 tiles (#2431), for a simple shingle-style roof. You can stagger the bottom edge and vary the color for more interest.

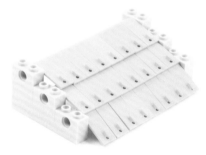

You can also stagger other thin pieces, like flippers (#2599), 2x3 pentagonal tiles (#22385), and even 1x3x1 doors (#3821/#3822).

Decorative Shingles

Mix plates, tiles, slopes, and plants to give your roof some character.

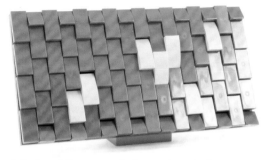

Mix in white curved slopes to mimic snow.

Place tiles on 3x4 tiles with 4 studs (#88646) to create a slightly corrugated pattern.

You can also create a corrugated pattern by staggering pins with friction ridges (#2780).

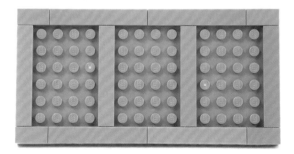

Use tiles on large plates to create panels.

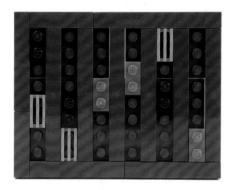

Plates or tiles in sand green and dark orange make the roof look old and weathered.

Curved Shingles

Mix colors and leave the bottom edge
uneven for more interest.

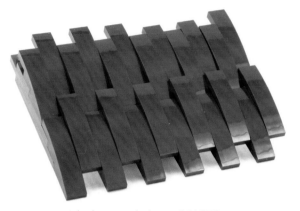

1x4 curved slope #61678

Alternate directions to create a
geometric pattern.

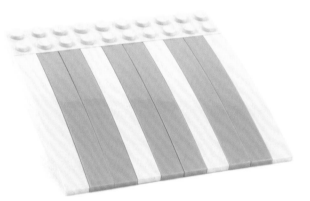

1x10 curved slope #85970

The underside of the 1x6 curved slope (#42022)
has many notches, which you can use to stack
these pieces in irregular ways.

Offset Shingles

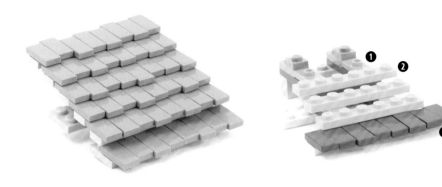

You can offset shingles by half a stud with jumper plates so that each row is one-and-a-half studs set back from the next. Because a 1x2 tile is open on the bottom, the tiles can be placed anywhere on the stud below for a randomized effect.

❶ 1x2 jumper plate #3794/#15573
❷ 1x plate (can be any length)
❸ 1x2 tile #3069

The yellow plates are 1x8, so the offset rows between them have to be one stud shorter (7 studs long) to accommodate the offset.

❶ 1x1 brick with studs on 4 sides #4733
❷ 1x8 plate #3460
❸ 1x8 brick #3008
❹ 4x8 plate #3035
❺ 1x3 plate #3623
❻ 1x4 plate #3710
❼ 1x2 tile #3069

You can also stagger tiles around the edge of a roof. This technique uses alternating raised tiles, along with flush tiles and layered tiles that are only partially attached.

Fixed-Angle Bases

Build a fixed base for your shingled roofs and other plate-based roof techniques.

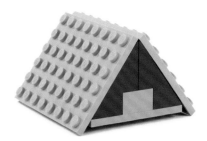

Attach plates directly onto
3x1x3 1/3 studded slopes (#6044).

Use a plane tail (#2340)
to support the roof plates.

Alternate these triangular pieces, 2x4 plates
with bottom struts to pins (#42608), so that the
roof plates can attach on both sides.

These asymmetric support legs (#30211) provide a surprisingly firm base for a roof.

4x4 modified facet brick #14413

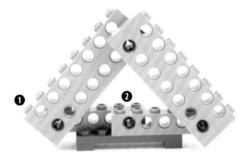

❶ 1x8 Technic brick #3702

❷ 1x6 Technic brick #3894

Fix the angle of your roofs by using 2x4 hinge plates (#3639 with #3640) to lock in the plates at the top.

❶ 2x2 plate with pin on bottom #2476

❷ 5x5 right angle Technic brick #32555

Lay garage roller door sections (#4218) over 4x8x2 1/3 castle turret tops (#6066).

- ❶ 1x2 modified plate with handle on side #2540
- ❷ 1x2 brick with 2 studs on side #11211
- ❸ 1x2 plate #3023
- ❹ Technic brick with 2 holes #32000
- ❺ 1x3 thin liftarm #6632

- ❶ 1x2 - 2x2 bracket #44728
- ❷ 1x2 tile #3069
- ❸ 1x2 brick with 2 studs on side #11211
- ❹ 1x2 brick with handle on side #30236
- ❺ 1x2 thin liftarm #41677

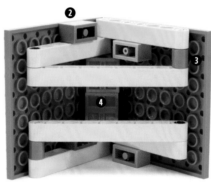

- ❶ 1x7 liftarm #32524
- ❷ 1x2 brick with 2 pins #30526
- ❸ 1L pin connector #18654
- ❹ 1x2 Technic pin connector plate #32530

How To: Masonry Bricks

Angle a 1x4 plate to fit into the grooves of 1x2 or 1x4 masonry profile bricks attached to a brick with studs on the side.

- ❶ 1x2 (or 1x4) modified brick with masonry profile #98283 (#15533)
- ❷ 1x4 brick with 4 studs on side #30414
- ❸ 1x4 plate #3710
- ❹ 2x6 plate #3795

Flexible-Angle Bases

Use clips, handles, hinge bricks, and Technic parts to build a more flexible base for your roofs.

Clips can support a roof plate from the top or the bottom.

❶ 1x2 plate with handle on side #48336

❷ 1x2 plate with clip on top #92280

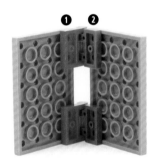

❶ 1x2 plate with handle on side #48336

❷ 1x2 plate with 2 clips #60470

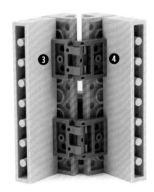

The clips can also be mounted in the middle.

❶ 1x1 cheese slope #54200

❷ 2x8 plate #3034

❸ 1x2 plate with 2 clips #60470

❹ 1x2 plate with handle on side #48336

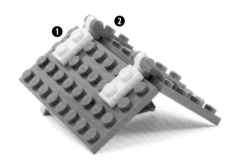

The clips can also be mounted on the outside of the roof.

❶ 1x2 plate with handle on side #48336

❷ 1x2 plate with 2 clips #60470

❶ 1x2 plate with clip horizontal on end #63868

❷ 1x2 modified plate with handle on end #60478

Some 1x2 plates with rail (#32028) help hold this angle in place.

Ball and socket joints work well as hinges.

❶ 1x2 modified plate with socket on side #14704

❷ 1x2 plate with ball on side #14417

Roof plates rest on slopes that look like rafters. You can use a plate with rail to catch the top of the slope that sticks up (red roof), or use it as a gutter (green roof).

❶ 1x2 plate with rail #32028

❷ 1x8 plate with rail #4510

❸ Short Technic slope #2743

Hinge Bricks

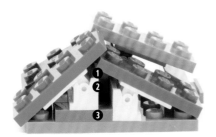

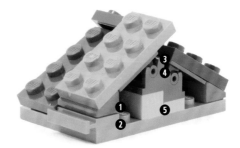

Use a jumper plate to give the roof a slight overhang (left) or place the hinge brick directly on stud to make the roof plate flush with the edge of the base (right).

❶ 2x2 hinge brick top #6134

❷ 1x2 hinge brick base #3937

❸ 1x2 jumper plate #3794/#15573

Rest the roof plate on cheese slopes.

❶ 1x2 cheese slope #85984

❷ 1x2 plate with rail #32028

❸ 2x2 hinge brick top #6134

❹ 1x2 hinge brick base #3937

❺ 1x2 plate #3023

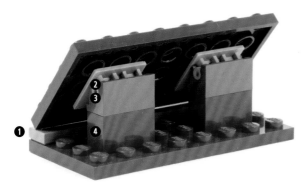

For a steeper pitch, stack the hinge bricks on regular bricks and then use tiles to hide the studs of the base.

❶ 1x2 tile #3069

❷ 2x2 hinge brick top #6134

❸ 1x2 hinge brick base #3937

❹ 1x2 brick #3004

Rest the hinge top on the inner row of slopes. The roof plate rests on the front slope for a secure fit.

❶ 1x2 cheese slope #85984

❷ 2x8 plate #3034

❸ 2x2 hinge brick top #6134

❹ 1x2 hinge brick base #3937

Technic Parts

You can extend an axle from wall to wall and rest your roof on the axle.

❶ 1x2 Technic brick with axle hole #32064

Liftarms work like hinges to hold plates together.

❶ 1x2 thin liftarm #41677
❷ 1x2 modified plate with handle on side #2540

❶ 1x2 thin liftarm #41677
❷ 3mm rigid hose #75
❸ 1x1 plate with ring #4081

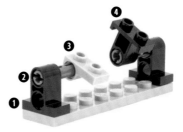

The pivot points of pin holes can be used to create an angle. Both pins and axles work.

❶ 1x4 Technic brick #3701
❷ 2x2 plate with 2 pin holes #2817
❸ 2x2 plate with 1 pin hole #2444
❹ 1x2 brick with pin #2458
❺ 1x2 Technic brick #3700
❻ Axle pin with 2L axle #18651
❼ 1x2 Technic pin connector plate #32530
❽ 1x2 Technic brick with axle hole #32064

Plates with pin holes can hold roof plates in position.

❶ 1x2 Technic pin connector plate #32530
❷ 3L pin #6558/#32556
❸ 1x2 plate with pin hole on bottom #18677
❹ 1x2 Technic pin connector plate with 1 hole #32529

Technic Gable Roofs

Use Technic pieces to create simple gable roofs.

1. #1 angled axle connector #32013
2. 2L axle connector #6538
3. #6 angled axle connector #32014

Mix in bushes and other Technic connectors to add more visual interest to your roof.

1x3 thin liftarm #6632

3x5 thin liftarm with quarter ellipse #32250

1. Technic axle towball #2736
2. #3 angled axle connector #32016
3. #5 angled axle connector #32015

1. 1x3 liftarm #32523
2. 1x9 liftarm #40490
3. 1x9 bent liftarm #32271

Thatched Roofs

Re-create more organic-looking roofs using the side edges of plates or by joining other stick-like pieces.

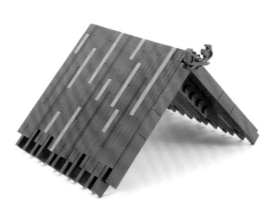

This technique primarily requires plates, except at the edges where tiles are used to cover up studs.

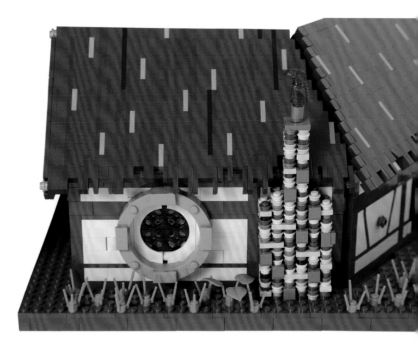

Combine bars with U-Clips to create rows of thatch.

❶ 4L bar #30374

❷ U-Clip (by BrickArms)

❸ 1L bar with clip mechanical claw #48729

Layer 4x4 rounded corner plates (#30565) to create a softer edge, which can be used to finish off the ridgeline.

Terra-cotta Roofs

You can also stack curved pieces to look like the clay tiles used in terra-cotta roofs.

1x2x1 1/3 modified brick
with curved top #6091

2x3 modified brick with
curved top #6215

1x3x2 arch with curved top #6005

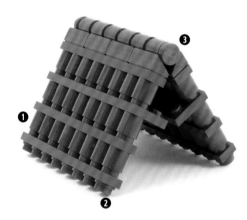

Alternate rows of plates and 1x1 round bricks.

❶ 1x1 round brick #3062

❷ 1x1 round plate #4073

❸ 1x1 round tile #98138

Cones in alternating orientation nest nicely and
can be attached to clips on top or bottom.

❶ 1x1 cone #4589

❷ 4L bar #30374

❸ 1x1 plate with horizontal clip #61252

Terra-cotta Neck Gables

You can insert rows of 2L pin connectors (#75535) between two gables to mimic the texture of terra-cotta roofing.

Or use round bricks and plates, mixing in extra plates as mortar to adjust the length as necessary. Use 1x4 plates (#3710) to connect the two sides so the rows don't slide down.

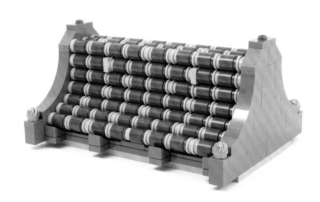

Terra-cotta Hip Roofs

You'll need at least one supporting plate to hold round bricks and cones together, but you can add in smaller plates to make your roof sturdier.

❶ 1x2 hinge brick #3937 with #3938

❷ 1x2 plate with 2 clips #60470

❸ 1x2 plate with handle on side #48336

Wedge Plate Roofs

Because the point of a symmetrical wedge plate or a pair of left and right wedge plates is two studs wide, these pieces are well suited to creating flat-top roofs.

3x6 wedge plates left/right #54384/#54383

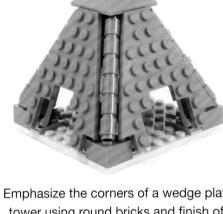

Emphasize the corners of a wedge plate tower using round bricks and finish off the top with slopes.

Larger wedges can accommodate larger roofs.

❶ 2x4 wedge plate left/right #41770/#41769

❷ 3x12 wedge plate left/right #47397/#47398

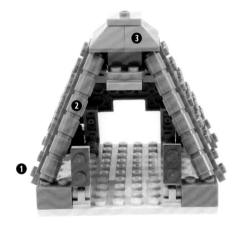

❶ 8x8 wedge plate with 3x4 cutout #6104

❷ 1x1 round brick #3062

❸ 2x2 double convex slope #3045

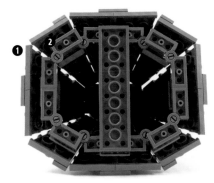

Wedge plates on hinge plates form an octagonal roof held together by a 2x8 plate (#3034) on the bottom. Use a shield to top it off.

❶ 3x6 wedge plate left/right #54384/#54383

❷ 1x4 hinge plate #2429 with #2430

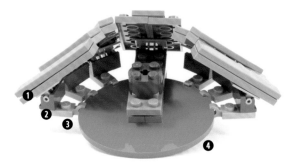

Use clip plates around a round tile to create a more circular roof and then finish off with a dish.

❶ 2x2 hinge brick top #6134

❷ 1x2 hinge brick base #3937

❸ 1x2 plate with clip horizontal on end #63868

❹ 8x8 round tile #6177

Another variation creates a circle using interconnecting hinge plates.

❶ 1x2 modified plate with handle on end #60478

❷ 1x2 plate with clip horizontal on end #63868

❸ 1x4 hinge plate #2429 with #2430

Curved Roofs

You can use arches and other round pieces to make both concave and convex curved roofs.

❶ 4x6x2/3 quad curved wedge #98281

❷ 4x6x1 2/3 trunk lid #4238

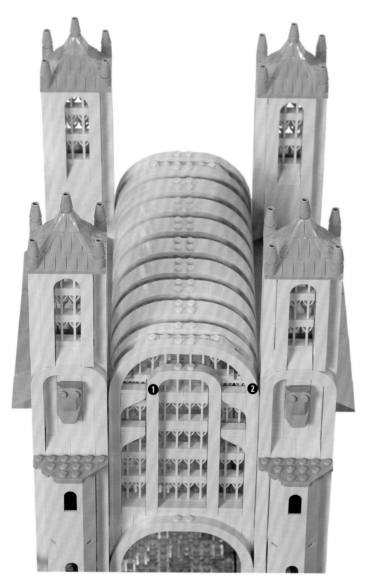

❶ 1x6x2 arch with curved top #6183

❷ 1x12x5 arch with curved top #6184

4x4x2 curved slope #61487

Raise alternating arches by a plate.

Create a pattern by alternating inverted arches (#18653) with curved bricks (#33243).

Finish the look with a contrasting color on each raised end.

Use an accent color to emphasize offset arches.

4x4x6 quarter cylinder #30562

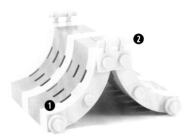

❶ 4x4 macaroni #48092

❷ 1x2 modified plate with handle on side #2540

❶ Garage roller door section #4218

❷ 1x5x4 inverted arch #30099

❶ 1x4 hinge brick #3830 with #3831

❷ 1x5x4 inverted arch #30099

❶ 1x5x4 inverted arch #30099

❷ 8x8x2 double curved slope #54095

❸ 4x4 macaroni #48092

Domed Roofs
and Spires

Round Roofs

Stack dishes to create low-profile roofs on top of round buildings.

6x6 quarter dish #95188

8x8 dish #3961

6x6x2 round corner brick #87559

8x8 dish #3961

10x10 quarter dish #58846

Join two 4x8x2 1/3 castle turret tops (#6066) to make an octagonal roof.

Stack dishes of various sizes.

Layer a 6x6 umbrella (#4094) on top of the Belville umbrella (#6252).

Basic Domes

Domes come in all sizes and shapes. They are an easy way to add curves to your roofs.

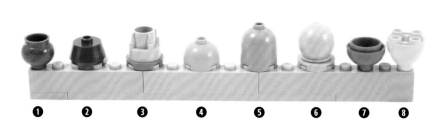

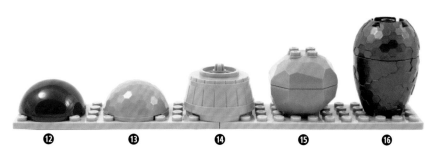

❶ Utensil pot #98374

❷ 2x2 truncated cone #98100

❸ Technic driving ring extension #32187

❹ 2x2 round brick dome top #553

❺ 2x2x1 2/3 round brick dome top #30151

❻ 2x2x2 crystal ball #30106

❼ 2x2 round brick dome bottom #15395

❽ 2x2 round brick dome bottom with studs #24947

❾ Rock arctic top #30286
Rock arctic bottom #30342

❿ 4x4x1 2/3 faceted pod #13754

⓫ 4x4x1 2/3 dragon egg top #24132
4x4x1 2/3 dragon egg bottom #24130

⓬ 4x4 cylinder hemisphere #86500

⓭ 4x4 multifaceted cylinder hemisphere #30208

⓮ Large half barrel #64951

⓯ Rock boulder top #30293
Rock boulder bottom #30294

⓰ 4x4x1 2/3 faceted pod #13754
4x4x3 faceted pod #11598

⓱ 3x3x2 dome corner #88293

⓲ 6x6x3 windscreen half-sphere canopy #50747

⓳ 3x6x5 bubble windscreen #30366

❶ 2x2 flower #4728/#98262

❷ 2x2 dish #4740

❸ 3x3 dish #43898

❹ 3x3x2 dome corner #88293

❶ Duplo cupcake top #98217

❷ Duplo muffin cup #98215

❸ Duplo waffle cone #15577

Use this green 11x11 dome (#98107)
to re-create an oxidized copper dome.

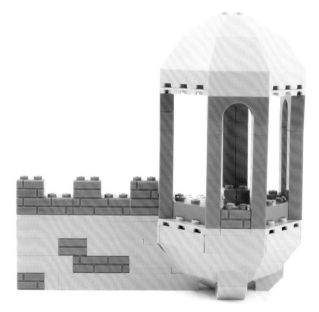

Top off a turret made from a 10x10x4
octagonal cockpit (#2618) with the matching
10x10x4 octagonal canopy (#2598).

Curved Slope Domes

Use various curved slopes and windscreen pieces to add interesting texture or patterns to your domed roofs.

1x3 curved slope #50950

1x4 curved slope #61678

1x6 curved slope #42022

1x3x2 curved brick #33243

1x6 curved slope #42022

3x4 triple wedge #64225

4x1 double curved slope #93273

Short Technic slope #2743

1x3x2 arch with curved top #6005

8x4x2 windscreen #30536

6x2x2 windscreen #92474

Wedge Plate Domes

Use the many different types of wedge plates to create a variety of domed roof shapes.

6x6 hexagonal plate #27255

2x4 wedge plate #51739

3x12 wedge plate left/right #47397/#47398

Brick-built Domes

You can also create domes using bricks and plates. You may want the aid of online LEGO rendering software to virtually construct larger domes before you build.

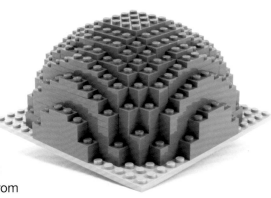

These two domes are exactly the same scale, but because the gray one is built from plates, it has subtler curves.

How To: Lowell Sphere

The Lowell Sphere is a special brick-built dome that uses studs on all sides to create a sphere made entirely of plates.

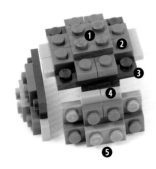

❶ 2x2 plate #3022

❷ 2x2 corner plate #2420

❸ 1x4 plate #3710

❹ 1x2 jumper plate #3794/#15573

❺ 1x2 plate #3023

Tower Roofs

You can use the premade 6x8x9 tower roof (#33215) alone, in pairs, or with other roof shapes.

Create a tower by combining the tower roof with 3x3x6 corner panels (#87421/#2345).

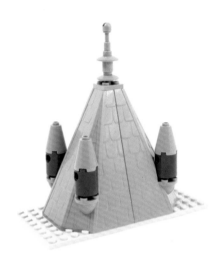

Use a tower roof by itself or in pairs.

Attach the tower roof to 10x10 quarter dishes (#58846) to cover a round tower.

Cone Spires

Use a single cone or stack several cones to make a simple spire.

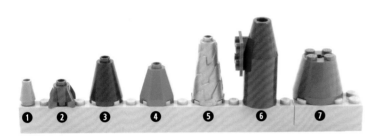

① 1x1 cone #4589

② 1x1 round brick with fins #4588

③ 2x2x2 cone #3942

④ 2x2x1 2/3 octagonal cone #6039

⑤ 2x2x3 jagged cone drill #28598

⑥ Engine with top plate #4868

⑦ 3x3x2 cone #6233

6x3x6 cone half #18909

① 1x1 round tile #98138

② 2x2x2 cone #3942

③ 4x4x2 hollow cone #4742

④ Flanged wheel #64712

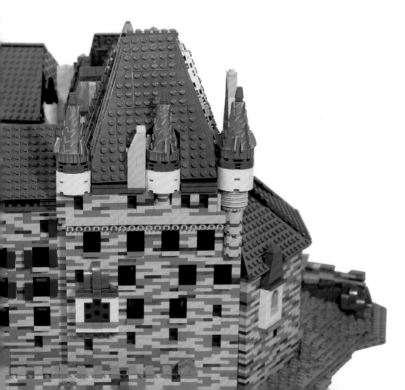

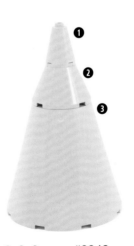

① 2x2x2 cone #3942

② 4x4x2 cone #3943

③ 8x4x6 cone half #47543

① 2x2x2 cone #3942

② 2x2 modified facet brick #87620

③ 1x1 plate with ring #4081

Slope Spires

These techniques require studs on all four sides of the interior structure and can be used for both round and square roofs.

2x4 slope #30363

4x2 triple wedge right #43711

6x2 wedge left #41748

1x6 curved slope #42022

1x2 triple slope #3048/#15571

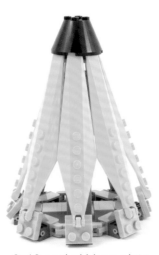

3x12 angled hinge plate #57906

1x2 modified plate with flexible tip #61406

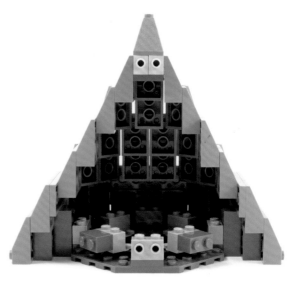

2x3 slope #3298

Ornamental Domes and Spires

Use curved pieces like blades and animal parts to create fun ornamental domes and spires.

Claw with clip #16770

Weapon crescent blade #98141

Ornamental fish #x59

Bony leg #15107

Elephant tail/trunk #43892

Khopesh sword #93247

Rounded double flame #18396pb03

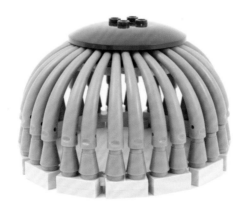

Dinosaur tail #40379

Flame #18395

Roof Decorations

Roof Ridges

Add in decorative elements to make a roof ridge more detailed and interesting.

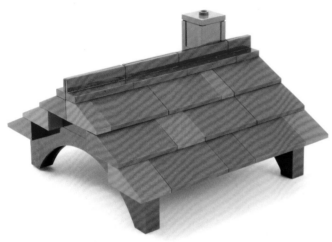

Even a simple panel ridge adds interest to a roof.

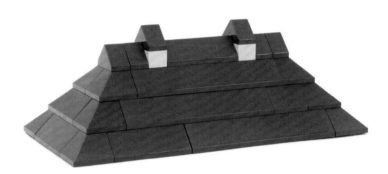

Raise a section of the ridge to look like vents.

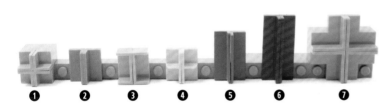

Use panels to line the tops of your roofs.

❶ 1x1x1 corner panel #6231

❷ 1x2x1 panel #4865

❸ 1x2x1 panel with 2 sides #23969

❹ 1x2x1 panel with center divider #93095

❺ 1x3x1 panel #23950

❻ 1x4x1 panel #30413

❼ 2x2x1 corner panel #91501

1x2 inverted double slope #3049

❶ 1x2 triple slope #3048

❷ 2x4 double slope #3041

❸ 1x1 cone #4589

1x2 double slope #3044

2x4 double slope #3041

2x2 curved top brick with
2 studs #30165

1x4x1 1/3 modified brick
with curved top #6191

Pneumatic hose T #4697

Toy winder key #98375

Ice cream cone #11610

Spear tip #24482

Claw #87747

Light cover #58176

1x1 cone #4589

3x3 corner plate #30357

Ornamental fish #x59

Pantograph shoe #2922

Bionicle back blade #44146

Gable Ends

The gable end is the wall area that encloses the end of a pitched roof. It is typically triangular but can vary depending on the shape of your roof.

Create an overhang by adding an extra row of slopes. You can also change the roof's pitch by using different types of slopes.

Create a stepped parapet and use a 1x2 plate with rail (#32028) and 1x2 cheese slope (#85984) for emphasis.

1x2 modified brick with groove #4216

1x2 plate with rail #32028

Turntable base #3680

4x4 rounded corner plate #30565

3x3 thin liftarm with quarter ellipse #32249

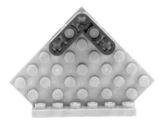

Attach a 3x3 thin L-shape liftarm (#32056) to a plate to add a gable vent.

Embellish with contrasting colors and lines.

Use shaped tiles to line the outer edges
of the gable end.

Alternate 1x1 bricks with
scroll (#20310) with slopes.

1x6x2 arch with curved top #6183

❶ 1x1 round plate with swirled top #15470

❷ 2x2 jumper plate #87580

❸ 1x3x3 arch #13965

Roof Trims

Here are some ways to line the rake edge of a roof to frame a gable end.

1x1 plate #3024

1x1 round plate #4073

12-tooth gear #6589

2x3x2/3 brick with wing end #47456

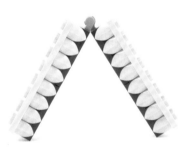

1x1 modified plate with
vertical tooth #15070

2x3 modified plate with hole #3176

Plant stem #15279

Lightsaber hilt #64567

1x8 plate with rail #4510

1x2 plate with handle on side #48336

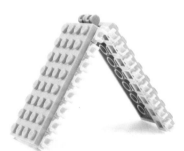

1x1 plate with vertical clip #4085

Rooftop Finials

Finials can add a bit of color or interest to a roof, spire, or tower.

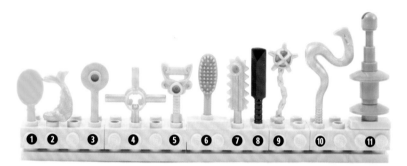

❶ Mirror #93080

❷ Ornamental fish #x59

❸ Signal paddle #3900

❹ Technic axle hub #48723

❺ Ornate key #19118

❻ Hairbrush #3852

❼ Chainsaw blade #6117

❽ Cricket bat (by BrickArms)

❾ Spiked flail #59232

❿ Snake #98136

⓫ 2x2 dish #4740
1x1 round brick #3062
Telescope #64644
Small lever base #4592

⓬ Technic ball joint #32474

⓭ Oval perfume bottle #6932

⓮ Light cover #58176

⓯ Ice cream scoops #6254

⓰ Ice cream cone #11610

⓱ Statuette #90398

⓲ Lipstick #93094

⓳ Telescope #64644

⓴ Sai weapon #98139

㉑ 1x2x2/3 modified brick with studs on sides #4595

㉒ Lantern (by BrickWarriors)

❶ Feathered wing #11100

❷ Chicken #95342

❸ Microfig #85863
Microfig helmet #94162

❹ Baby dragon #41535

❺ Paw #15090

❻ Scallop shell #18970

Weather Vanes

Weather vanes are a great way to add a bit of character to a roof. They can be made by attaching all sorts of small decorative pieces to long bar pieces.

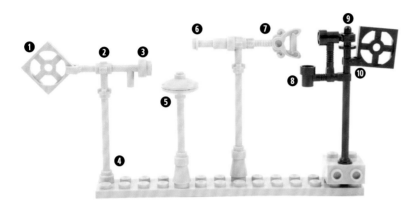

❶ Turntable base #3680

❷ Handle with side studs #92690

❸ Space gun/torch #3959/#86208

❹ 1x4 antenna #3957

❺ 2x2 dish #4740

❻ Telescope #64644

❼ Ornate key #19118

❽ 1x3 bar with clip and stud #4735

❾ 8L bar with stop rings and pin #2714

❿ U-Clip (by BrickArms)

Drains and Downspouts

Drains and downspouts fit nicely into corners and can also break up a wall section. Extra detail can be added with decorative parts that connect the structure to the wall.

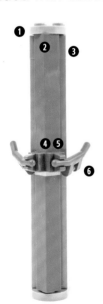

❶ 2x3 modified plate with hole #3176

❷ 1x1x5 brick #2453

❸ 1x2x5 brick #2454

❹ 1x1 tile with clip #2555

❺ 1x1 brick with stud on 2 adjacent sides #26604

❻ Handlebars #30031

❶ #4 angled axle connector #32192

❷ 2L Technic pin connector #62462

❸ Handcuffs #61482

❹ Nozzle #60849

Dormers

A dormer is a window that juts out from a sloping roof. Here are some ideas for integrating dormers into your roofs.

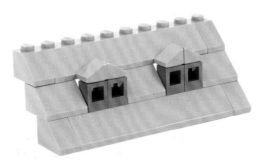

Use the square opening on the back of a 1x1 headlight brick (#4070) to make a small roof vent or window by capping it with a 1x1 cheese slope (#54200).

Regular 1x1 bricks (#3005) in a contrasting color can also create a vent dormer to break up a large roof surface.

When working with small dormers, you can use windows with or without a brick frame. The dormer on the right is capped with a 2x4 triple wedge (#47759).

To fill the gap between the roofline and the window frame, use a second empty frame behind the first.

Add a hood over the dormer with a differently angled slope—in this case, a 5x8x2/3 curved slope (#15625).

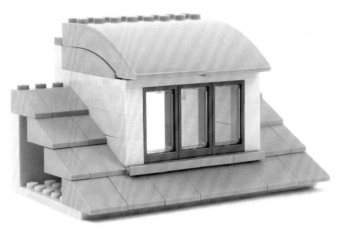

Curved dormer roofs, like this one constructed from 8x4x2 curved windscreens (#46413) on 1x6 curved slopes (#42022), make a nice contrast against a roof of regular slopes.

You can also place a dormer where the wall transitions to the roof.

Use a contrasting color for the wall so it stands out against the roof.

You can use any "material" or shape for the dormer roof—it doesn't have to match the rest of the roof.

4x2 triple wedge left #43710

4x2 triple wedge right #43711

4x4 round corner brick #2577

7x3 flag with rod #30292

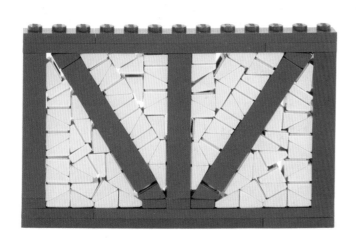

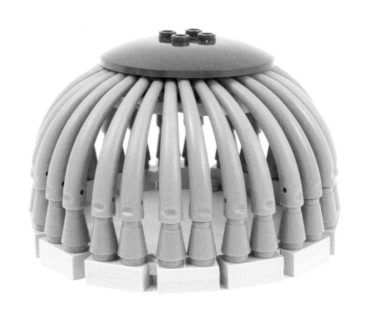

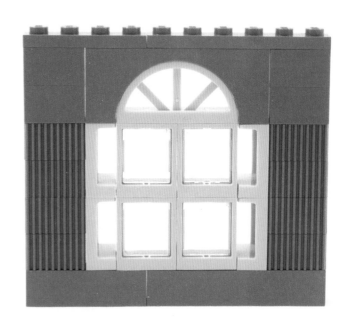